THE BEATLES' INVASION OF CANADA

OUR HEARTS WENT BOOM

Brian Kendall

AUG 1 3 2002   VIKING

VIKING

Published by the Penguin Group

Penguin Books Canada Ltd, 10 Alcorn Avenue, Toronto, Ontario, Canada M4V 3B2

Penguin Books Ltd, 27 Wrights Lane, London W8 5TZ, England

Viking Penguin, a division of Penguin Books USA Inc., 375 Hudson Street, New York, New York 10014, U.S.A.

Penguin Books Australia Ltd, Ringwood, Victoria, Australia

Penguin Books (NZ) Ltd, cnr Rosedale and Airborne Roads, Albany, Auckland 1310, New Zealand

Penguin Books Ltd, Registered Offices: Harmondsworth, Middlesex, England

First published 1997

1 3 5 7 9 10 8 6 4 2

Printed and bound in Canada on acid-free paper ∞

CANADIAN CATALOGUING IN PUBLICATION DATA

Kendall, Brian
  Our hearts went boom: the Beatles' invasion of Canada

ISBN 0-670-87689-5

1. Beatles – Journeys – Canada. 2. Beatles – Public opinion. 3. Rock music – Canada – 1961–1970 – History and

criticism. 4. Rock music – Great Britain – 1961–1970 – History and criticism. I. Title.

ML421.B4K33 1997   782.42166'092'2   C97-930395-8

Visit Penguin Canada's web site at **www.penguin.ca**

For Sharon,
born in the year of
the great Beatles invasion

Contents

OUR HEARTS WENT BOOM

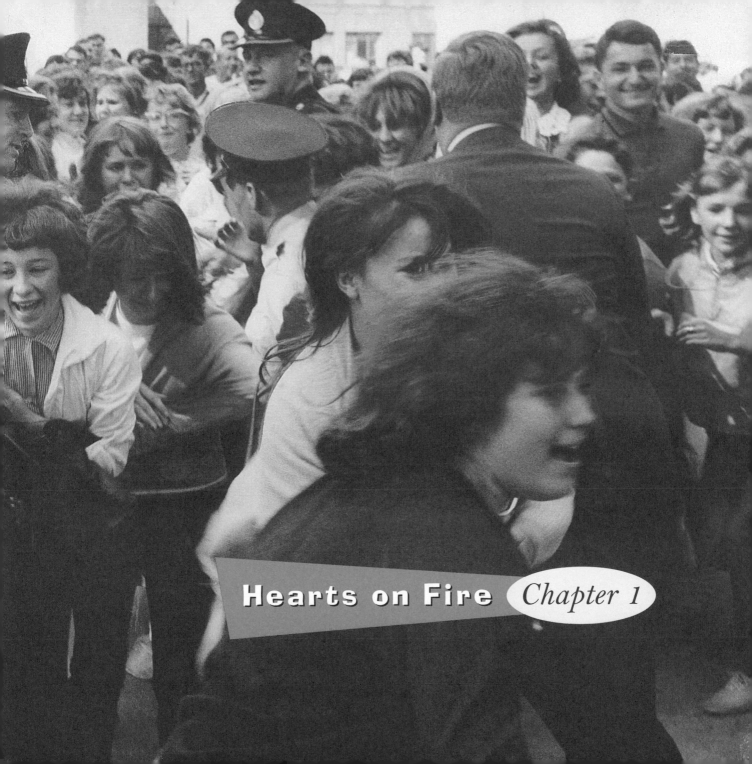

Hearts on Fire *Chapter 1*

THEY CAME, George Harrison said, to save the world
from boredom – and millions of adolescents zealously
embraced the cure. No one old enough to remember will
ever forget the hysteria preceding the Beatles' historic live
North American television debut on "The Ed Sullivan Show."

Day and night, rock 'n' roll radio stations played almost
nothing but their songs. "I Want to Hold Your Hand," the
Beatles' first hit on this side of the Atlantic, sold a quarter of a
million copies in three days following its release in early
January of 1964. Less than two weeks later it had soared past
the million mark. In February, the Beatles accounted for an
unprecedented sixty per cent of all records purchased in Canada
and the United States.

Dozens of Beatle products – from bath mats and drum sets

to hand bags, brooches, pendants, perfume and nylon stockings patterned with tiny Beatle faces – flooded the market. One Toronto wig-maker sold eighty Beatle wigs in a single month. A far cheaper version endorsed by the band and guaranteed to fit all head sizes sold by the thousands.

Across Canada, teenage boys started combing their hair down in front, Beatle-style. Outraged school principals banned the look because of its so-called disruptive influence. Four boys attending Ottawa's Lisgar Collegiate were ordered to comb their hair differently or stay at home. The principal at Vancouver's St. George's school told an offender that he could keep the new style if he also wore short pants to show how immature he was. F. L. Burnham, principal of Sir Winston Churchill School in Vancouver, explained that he couldn't permit anything outlandish that might cause giggling and other foolery in class.

No act in entertainment history had ever made this type of impact – not Frank Sinatra, not even Elvis Presley when he exploded onto the scene several years before.

At last, on Friday, February 7, the Beatles' plane touched down in New York. When they looked out and saw thousands of frenzied youngsters on the airport observation deck, they thought the president of the United States or some other world celebrity must also have landed. Only Charles Lindbergh, almost forty years before, had received so fervent an airport reception.

During a raucous press conference held minutes after they landed, North Americans got their first exposure to the droll, often rude, uniquely Liverpudlian charm that had

5

ABOVE:
Though produced by the thousands, Beatle wigs in their original packaging can nowadays fetch upwards of $150.

BELOW:
The boys charm the press in New York minutes after their historic arrival on February 7, 1964.

already helped Beatlemania sweep Britain and most of Europe.

In his thickest Scouse accent, John Lennon shouted "Shaaaaaarup!" to quiet the crowd.

"How do you like this welcome?" someone asked.

"So this is America," Ringo Starr said as he looked around the packed lounge. "They all seem out of their minds."

"Are you going to get a haircut?" shouted a reporter to gales of laughter.

"We had one yesterday," John answered.

"What about the campaign in Detroit to stamp out the

The Beatles' live performance on Ed Sullivan's Sunday night variety show drew the largest audience to that point in television history.

6

Beatles?"

"We've got a campaign of our own to stamp out Detroit," shot back Paul McCartney.

"Does all the adulation from teenage girls affect you?"

"When I feel my head start to swell," said John, "I look at Ringo and know perfectly well we're not supermen."

"Was your family in show business?" a reporter asked John.

"Well," he leered, "me dad used to say me mother was a great performer."

Two nights later on Ed Sullivan's variety show, the Beatles delivered awesomely assured, virtually pitch-perfect performances of five of their most famous songs: "All My Loving," "Till There Was You," "She Loves You," "I Saw Her Standing There" and "I Want to Hold Your Hand." Young girls from the Arctic to points south of the Mexican border wept uncontrollably in front of their TV sets. An estimated seventy-three million people tuned in, the largest audience to that point in television history.

Following a whirlwind fifteen-day visit that included two more appearances with Sullivan and rapturously received concerts in Washington and at New York's Carnegie Hall, the Beatles returned home to Britain. Soon afterward came the announcement that the Fab Four, as all the world knew them by now, would come back in August to start a more than month-long North American tour. A stop at Toronto's Maple Leaf Gardens was a certainty. Promoters in Vancouver and Montreal also hoped to secure concerts for their cities.

This Capitol Records ad from the back of a Montreal radio station's hit record list dates from January, 1964. Note the box at the bottom promoting the band's appearance on "The Ed Sullivan Show."

Delirious with excitement, Beatlemaniacs across the country impatiently began the long countdown to what became known as B-Day, or Beatles-Day, the date their heroes would first set foot on Canadian soil.

JOHN, PAUL, GEORGE AND RINGO HAD STRUCK A CHORD THAT resonates to this day. After their breakthrough performance on the Sullivan show, nothing was ever the same again. For aging baby boomers and even many of today's adolescents, the Beatles represent a golden age before the unwelcome advent of punk music, gangsta rap and grunge rock; a time of innocence when music still sounded sweet.

But though it starts with the music, their enduring appeal goes much deeper than that. "The Beatles represent a kind of youthful, hopeful state of mind," insists Peter Miniaci, the owner of Toronto's Beatlemania Shoppe, the only store in Canada devoted exclusively to products and memorabilia related to the band. "People constantly tell me how much the Beatles still mean to them; how they admire John Lennon's bed-in for peace, or how all four of them believed so completely in themselves and the integrity of their music. For a lot of people, the Beatles are still role models."

At age thirty-four, Miniaci is too young to have seen the Beatles perform live. "I almost feel as if I was there," he says wistfully. "I've heard so many stories about the Canadian concerts. They were such huge events in the lives of the people I meet. Everyone who was there seems to carry the experience with them."

Memorabilia collectors the world over vie for every scrap of Beatles history. At a Tokyo auction in March of 1997, a grey suit worn on stage by John Lennon brought $35,000 (U.S.), while Paul McCartney's custom-made bass guitar sold for

1964 — A-Bombs, Bullets and the Maple Leaf Forever

CHINA EXPLODED its first atomic bomb in 1964.... Soviet leader Nikita Krushchev was deposed in a Kremlin coup that had the world shaking in fear of what might come next....The U.S. bombed North Vietnam as the undeclared war continued to escalate....In South Africa, freedom fighter Nelson Mandela was thrown behind bars. Throughout a year filled with mostly bad news, Beatlemania lifted the spirits of a world beset by what often appeared to be insurmountable problems.

Canadians shouldered worries about the growing separatist movement in Quebec. That October, defiant crowds demonstrated during a visit by Queen Elizabeth and Prince Philip to Quebec City. Thirty-two people were arrested and several injured by club-wielding police.

Even Prime Minister Lester Pearson's quest to give Canada its own flag, which should have been a joyous event, was tainted by endless squabbling. Finally, on December 15, after a marathon thirty-three-day debate in the House of Commons, the government invoked closure and the country had a flag that its advocates hoped would symbolize a new and stronger Canada.

Whether they fully realized it or not, Canadians had a great deal to be thankful for in 1964. The economy was booming and almost everyone across the nation who wanted work could find it. A working man's wage was around $7,000, which might be enough to support an entire family. Three-bedroom houses in our largest cities cost about $15,000. At Simpson's, a two-trouser, wool suit sold for $72. Speedy Muffler would install a new muffler for $7.95. A one-pound bag of Maxwell House coffee cost 89 cents at IGA.

Canadians excelled in a variety of endeavours. The world applauded when a contingent of 1,150 of our troops led a United Nations force on a peace-keeping mission in Cyprus. Our four-man bobsled team captured the gold medal at the Winter Olympics. Northern Dancer, selected the outstanding individual Canadian sports performer of 1964, won the Kentucky Derby, the Preakness Stakes and the Queen's Plate before retiring to stud.

All this on top of the unforgettable thrill of the Beatles' concerts in Vancouver, Toronto and Montreal. For youngsters across Canada who couldn't make it, there were always the Fab Four's albums. Eaton's offered them on sale most of that year for $3.30 apiece.

Beatles manager Brian Epstein smoothed the band's rough edges and set the lads on the road to stardom.

$200,000. The final tally from the sale — billed as the first major rock 'n' roll auction devoted entirely to the Fab Four — came to $1.3 million.

Over three decades after they first topped the record charts, the Beatles remain the world's most popular band. Three "Anthology" volumes of out-takes and live recordings shot to number one in 1996, a year in which the group sold in excess of twenty million albums. That was more than any other pop group and even more, astonishingly enough, than they ever sold in any one year of the sixties.

According to Apple, the record label created by the Beatles, four out of every ten of those albums were purchased by children, teenagers and young adults who weren't even born when the band broke up.

ENGLISH TEENS HAD BEEN FULL-BLOWN Beatle fanatics for almost a year by the time the craze took hold over here. Born of working-class families in the hard-scrabble port city of Liverpool, the Beatles first began to gather a following at The Cavern, a hometown club located in the dank basement of a former fruit and vegetable warehouse.

Their prospects brightened late in 1961 when dapper, twenty-seven-year-old Brian Epstein, whose affluent family owned a Liverpool furniture and record store, became their manager. Convinced from the start that his wards were destined for stardom, Epstein insisted that the Beatles adopt a slicker, more professional image. Brushed-tweed grey lounge suits with pencil-thin lapels and matching ties replaced the black leather gear they had previously worn on stage. Pointy-toed boots with Cuban heels (famous as Beatle boots) completed the ensemble. The boys had already started wearing their hair longer and combing it forward before they met Epstein.

Early in 1963, the Beatles enjoyed their first number-one hit, the Lennon-McCartney composition "Please, Please Me," which in just four weeks rocketed, in the words of an ecstatic John Lennon, "right up to the toppermost of the poppermost."

Soon there were block-long line-ups, audiences of sobbing young girls, and often rioting in the streets wherever they performed throughout Britain. Doctors reported that many girls were having orgasms during the shows.

Few adult observers could fathom how the Beatles had managed it. Their music didn't seem catchier or in any other way more compelling than that of other performers then on the scene. Like most teenage fads, this one was bound to quickly fade away.

Even later, on this side of the ocean, many people still didn't get it. "They sounded unhip to me, a big scam, and I resisted being caught up in it," remembers Duff Roman, then a disc jockey with Toronto rock station CKEY. "They sounded like white boys doing a bad impression of black singers. Later on their music developed and you could appreciate their genius. But at first I wasn't too optimistic about where it was all going."

Social psychologists and historians have puzzled over the Beatles' amazing popularity ever since. Some have theorized that it was their long hair that initially gave them an edge over the competition. Because other adult males wore their

11

FLASHBACK TO '64...
January 6 — With his visit to Israel and Jordan, Pope Paul VI becomes the first pontiff to ride in an airplane and to travel to the Holy Land.

12

RIGHT:
Fan club president Trudy
Medcalf quickly became
Canada's most famous
Beatlemaniac. Here she's
pictured with DJ Dave Johnson,
her co-host for a popular radio
show on Toronto's CHUM.

BELOW:
Trudy's membership card for
Britain's Official Beatles
Fan Club.

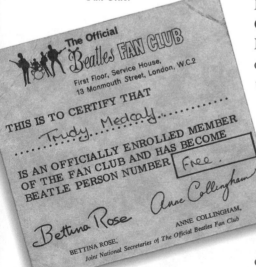

hair so much shorter, adolescents saw the longer style as something new and exclusive to the changing times, something they could claim as their own.

Or maybe it was mostly a matter of good timing. Weary of American domination of their radio and television sets, British teens were ready to embrace home-grown heroes. Cheering for the Liverpool Four was rather like rooting for mother England in an international football match. In turn, their success in North America might have been influenced by the pall cast by the recent assassination of President John F. Kennedy. In their wit, youth and high spirits, the Beatles offered a renewal of hope.

This last factor, the undeniable charm of the lads, can hardly be overstated. "The Beatles made me laugh immediately," wrote Maureen Cleave of the London *Evening Standard* after an interview early in 1963. "Their wit was just so keen and sharp – John Lennon, especially. They all had this wonderful quality. It wasn't innocent, but everything was new to them.... John Lennon has an upper lip which is brutal in a devastating way. George Harrison is handsome, whimsical, and untidy. Paul McCartney has a round baby face while Ringo Starr is ugly but cute. Their physical appearance inspires frenzy. They look beat-up and depraved in the nicest way."

Very young girls wanted to mother the Beatles; those slightly older may have desired much more, but most didn't dare speak of it in those more puritanical times. Adolescent females so identified with their favourite Beatle that many even modelled their personalities after them. A John girl was cheeky, cynical, rebellious and sarcastic. A George girl was dreamy and a little secretive. A Paul girl, meanwhile, was dutiful, an A-student, unfailingly polite and full of charm. And a Ringo girl, though probably not the best at

school work, was fun loving, earnest and liked by all.

The Beatles toured frantically throughout that summer of 1963. On July 1, they paused in London to record "She Loves You," destined to be their biggest hit yet.

"I first saw them later that month during a concert at Margate," remembers Trudy Medcalf, then a fourteen-year-old from Toronto visiting relatives in England. "All of my older cousins were just crazy about the Beatles. It was impossible not to get caught up in the excitement. Everyone was talking about them."

In a rise that paralleled that of her favourite band, Medcalf would quickly become Canada's most famous Beatlemaniac. After applying to the Official Beatles Fan Club ("I told them I was seventeen to make me seem more responsible"), she started an Ontario chapter back home in Toronto.

By the following January, the phone in her home rang

the
PAUNCH & TRUDY
show

BEATLEMANIA!
WITH THE BEATLES

...week nights at 8 p.m., DAVE JOHNSON
and TRUDY MEDCALF (president of the
only official Beatle Fan Club in Ontario)
present 30 minutes of BEATLE music and
news !!
★★★★★★★★★
CHUM Teen Product of the Week
Helps clear skin fast Clearasil

It took months for the Beatles' following to build in North America. Their first three releases in Canada, including "Love Me Do" and "From Me to You," together sold fewer than a thousand copies before their re-issue months later.

14

constantly and the mail brought more than one hundred letters a day. Then CHUM, Toronto's pre-eminent rock station, offered to help out by taking over all club correspondence and by printing official membership cards. Among her duties, Trudy edited a newsletter every two months or so.

At its peak, membership totalled more than ninety thousand, making it the largest officially sanctioned Beatles fan club outside of Britain. Medcalf's celebrity grew even larger when CHUM hired her to co-host the Paunch and Trudy Show, with DJ Dave Johnson (known as "Paunch" because of his oversized belly). "We'd record a week's worth of shows every Friday night after school," she recalls. "Because of my position with the fan club, I received a lot of inside information from Britain about things like their upcoming albums and the Beatles' plans to tour or make a movie. We'd play records and I'd talk about what I'd heard.

"Everything about the Beatles was so new, so upbeat," Medcalf says. "They had such tremendous energy. Looking back, I sometimes think it was as if they were fated to happen."

On October 10, 1963, the Beatles collected their first gold record when confirmation came that sales of "She Loves You" had passed the million mark. Just three days later their popularity soared even higher with a nationally televised appearance on Val Parnell's "Sunday Night at the London Palladium," the nation's top-rated variety show.

Screaming "We Want the Beatles," a mob of two thousand girls battled police outside the theatre. Inside, besotted teens hurled themselves against the line of bobbies guarding the stage. Police vans cordoned off the front of the theatre so that the Beatles could be smuggled to safety.

The next morning an unknown Fleet Street headline writer coined a new term that perfectly captured the insanity:

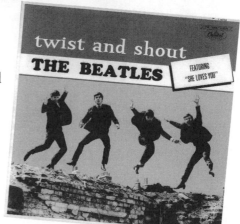

Beatlemania.

By this point all of Britain was smitten. "You have to be a real sour square not to love the nutty, noisy, happy, handsome Beatles. If they don't sweep your blues away, brother, you're a lost cause," editorialized the *Daily Mirror*, which just months before had dismissed the Fab Four as "the pimple of the month."

And yet even now there were those who believed the Beatles' magic could never be successfully exported across the Atlantic. No English act had ever conquered America, the cradle of rock 'n' roll. All through the past year executives at Capitol Records in Los Angeles, the American subsidiary of the Beatles' parent label, EMI, had stubbornly declined its option to distribute the group's records in the United States. Their sound wasn't right, they said. American teens wouldn't get it. Consequently, the Beatles' first singles, released by small independent labels, had disappeared without a trace.

But north of the border in Toronto there was at least one Capitol executive convinced of the Beatles' destiny. British-born Paul White, in charge of both signing new talent and handling national promotion for Capitol Records of Canada, first heard a Beatles recording in January while going through a pile of samples sent from the British head office. "I used to listen to about fifty new records a week," he remembers. "Then one day I put on "Love Me Do" by a group called the Beatles. I

Packaged by Capitol Records of Canada, these three Beatles albums were sold only in Canada.

15

Capitol Canada record executive Paul White was among the first to champion the band on this side of the Atlantic. Here White (hand on George's shoulder) is pictured with other Capitol executives during the Beatles' first visit to Toronto.

immediately sat up and took notice. The sound was so different, so completely fresh.

"I'm certainly not going to claim that I could read the future and already knew how big the Beatles were going to be," White continues, "but I did like them a lot and wanted Capitol Canada to get in on the ground floor. I decided to release the Beatles' records in Canada."

There were times when White's bosses were ready to tear up the Beatles' contract. "Love Me Do," the band's first single in Canada, sold just one hundred and seventy copies. "Please, Please Me" fared little better. The Beatles' third release, "From Me to You," sold about five hundred copies.

"The president of Capitol Canada in those days had no clue about pop music," says White, who was thirty at the time. "All he understood, all he liked, was jazz. He'd get in these little digs at me about the Beatles' poor sales. But I knew something was starting to happen. Little girls would come into the office and ask if we had any photos of the Beatles. Our salesmen were starting to get excited, too. Still, it was touch and go to convince the company to hold on for just a while longer."

Then came the Beatles' luckiest break yet. On October 31, they returned to London following a triumphant tour of Sweden. Screeching thousands waited to greet them at Heathrow. Out in force was the British press, including more than a hundred reporters and a BBC television crew.

As fate would have it, Ed Sullivan was also on hand that day at Heathrow. Waiting to catch a flight to New York, he stared fascinated at the incredible scene through a terminal window. On the spot he decided to sign this British phenomenon for his show.

Beatlemania had become an irresistible force. With word of the Sullivan signing, North America scrambled to cash in. Red-faced Capitol executives in Los Angeles, finally admitting their mistake, hurriedly arranged the release of "I Want to Hold Your Hand" and the backlog of other Beatles songs. An unprecedented $50,000 was budgeted for an advertising blitz built around the slogan "The Beatles are Coming!"

Meanwhile, north of the border, Capitol Canada's record presses were already spinning out the hits.

FANATICAL FOOLS IN TORONTO PHONED A FAMILY NAMED BETLE at all hours to inquire if they were related to the Beatles. A Hamilton bakery could barely meet the demand for its special ninety-eight–cent Beatle cakes, scrumptious cupcake-like

FLASHBACK TO '64...
February 7 — Canadians win the Olympic four-man bobsled gold medal at Innsbruck.

creations adorned with vague likenesses of the band. Across Canada, teenagers impatiently awaited the arrival in stores of sixteen thousand rolls of Beatles wallpaper rushed over from Britain. "You've heard them, you've seen them – now you can even paper the walls with them."

Things might have been expected to calm down at least a little after the Beatles returned to London. But everything the four said or did made headlines. Many Canadian papers ran Beatles-related items almost daily. When nothing came in over the wire, editors would phone the local university and assign yet another eminent psychologist the task of trying to explain how it had all begun.

For weeks the Beatles dominated the record charts in a manner never seen before or since. Their supremacy reached a peak the week of March 23, 1964, when the Top-Fifty listing compiled by Toronto's CHUM showed them in possession of six of the top ten spots. Flip-sided hits "All My Loving" and "This Boy" topped the chart. Another double effort, "I Want to Hold Your Hand" and "I Saw Her Standing There," placed second. "She Loves You" was third. "Please, Please Me" took seventh. "Love Me Do" finished eighth. "From Me to You" rounded out the top ten.

The Beatles were a hit-making machine. Their newest single, "Can't Buy Me Love," which placed fourteenth in the CHUM listing, would rapidly climb to number one not only in Canada, but in at least twenty-two other countries around the world.

Around this time the Vancouver *Sun* printed a letter from teenager Lora Handsen of North Bend, British Columbia, who described how it felt to be completely wacky over the Beatles – or "Beatleized" as she put it. "I think Beatle, talk Beatle, walk Beatle and look

The Beatles' popularity reached a peak the week of March 23, 1964, when the Top-Fifty listing compiled by Toronto's CHUM showed them in possession of six of the top ten spots.

Beatle," she wrote. "It makes me feel happy and wonderful all the time…. I don't have a Beatle wig; I have the real thing – a Beatle hairdo…. I don't know what it is but ever since I turned Beatle, I feel like a new person."

Handsen also said that many people she met cruelly laughed at what they considered her silly attitude and appearance. "If you don't like us Beatlemaniacs," she pleaded, "don't scorn us but tolerate us because the Beatles are here to stay and so are we."

Popular comedians of the day – including Bob Hope, who

Fans began queuing outside Toronto's Maple Leaf Gardens seventy-three hours before tickets went on sale. Here early birds settle in for the duration outside the storied arena.

seemed especially fond of the gag – could reduce audiences to tears of laughter simply by donning a Beatle wig and singing or shouting "Yeah, Yeah, Yeah." Many adults still viewed Beatlemania as a joke or, worse still, feared it as something they didn't quite understand but instinctively knew to be subversive.

In Fenelon Falls, Ontario, a fifty-six-year-old man shot himself to death after an argument with his schoolteacher wife about one of her pupils' Beatle haircuts. He had been drunk when the argument flared, but already across the land many perfectly sober fathers were railing at long-haired sons to trim

With twenty-four hours still to go, the ticket line in Toronto already stretched several hundred feet down the sidewalk past the old Carlton movie theatre.

their locks or else. They were right to fear the influence of the Beatles. The revolution had begun.

ON A COLD AND RAINY WEDNESDAY MORNING IN APRIL, 1964, thousands of kids queued outside Maple Leaf Gardens to purchase tickets for the Toronto concert, scheduled for Labour Day, September 7. By that point a show had also been confirmed for the Forum in Montreal the next day. Negotiations for a Vancouver concert sometime in August were still under way.

First in line outside the Gardens' wickets was eighteen-year-old Robin Timmerman, who staked her place at the front early Sunday morning, seventy-three hours before the tickets were scheduled to go on sale. Accompanying her were her sister Jan, sixteen, and Adrienne, a seventeen-year-old girlfriend.

As the eldest, Robin, who worked as a file clerk in a downtown office, took the night shift, spending the long hours dozing in her sleeping bag, snacking on junk food and reading Beatles fan magazines by the flickering light of the Gardens' marquee. Her sister, who was still in school, took over for a few hours starting at dawn. Adrienne, who worked part-time evenings, held their place in line the rest of the day.

That first night, a dozen other teenagers took up positions behind Robin, but only four had the grit to last until morning. "I would have sat there for two weeks to get a good seat," Robin remembers. "What the MuchMusic generation might not understand is that back then we couldn't just put a Beatles video in a VCR and play it over and over again. The thought of actually seeing them perform was such a novelty that I didn't just want a ticket to the concert, I wanted to get the best seat in the house."

By Tuesday the line stretched several hundred feet along the sidewalk towards the old Carlton movie theatre, where the

ABOVE AND BELOW:
Rival radio stations CHUM and CKEY parked their mobile studio vans in adjacent lots outside the Gardens. DJs wandered the ticket line conducting on-the-spot interviews.

feature attraction was the screwball comedy *It's A Mad, Mad, Mad, Mad World*. Even cold temperatures and persistent rain didn't dampen the enthusiasm of the throng. Huddled together under umbrellas and sodden blankets, the kids turned up the volume of their transistor radios, passed along the potato chips and entertained themselves by harmonizing on Beatles songs.

Every day of the vigil the local papers gave the story front-page play. Rival radio stations CHUM and CKEY parked their mobile studio vans in adjacent lots for the duration. DJs wandered the ticket line conducting on-the-spot interviews.

FAR RIGHT:
Tension built as the hours counted down to the opening of the Gardens' ticket windows.

BELOW:
Determined to get the best seat in the house, eighteen-year-old Robin Timmerman stubbornly staked her place at the head of the line.

22

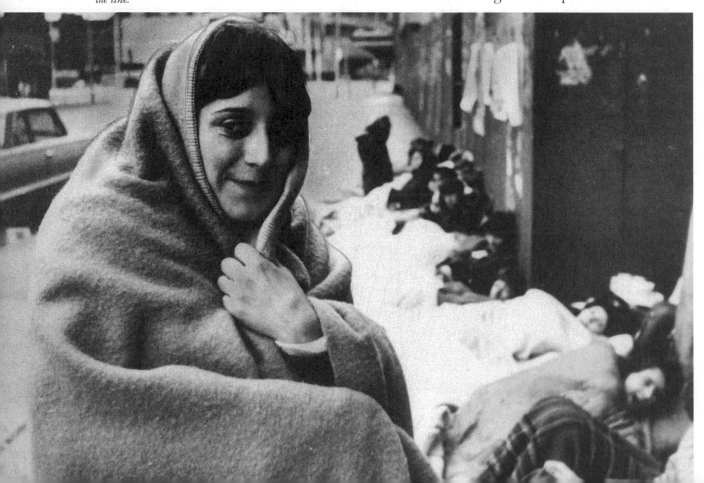

Of course, it didn't go unnoticed that most of the kids must have been skipping school to be there. Many of them turned away whenever a photographer raised his camera. Toronto Board of Education officials considered sending a truant officer to the scene. But they sensibly decided to leave the disciplining to school principals.

Smelling a photo opportunity, Stafford Smythe and Harold Ballard, president and executive vice-president of Maple Leaf Gardens, playfully donned Beatle wigs before venturing out onto the sidewalk at noon on Tuesday to serve cups of coffee and kibitz with about thirty young fans.

That night at the Gardens, the Toronto Maple Leafs played host to the Detroit Red Wings for the fifth game of a Stanley Cup final the home side would eventually win in seven. Fearing a mix-up with ticket-holders to the hockey game, police issued everyone in the Beatles line a numbered card and sent them home for the night. The card guaranteed their place the next morning.

Though it seemed incredible, the hullabaloo outside the storied arena over Beatles tickets at times threatened to overshadow the hockey playoffs. And this in a city where hockey had always been more religion than sport.

During a luncheon at the Gardens,

King Clancy, the Leafs' assistant general manager and resident leprechaun, told a suitably hushed audience, "You won't believe this, but we've had people offering to trade their Stanley Cup tickets – for *Beatles* tickets. It wouldn't be right, even if the Beatles were Irish."

No doubt acting on behalf of pleading grandchildren, Leaf hockey immortal Charlie Conacher reportedly called the Gardens' box office and said, "Never mind the Leafs, get me some Beatles tickets."

By Wednesday morning, with the ticket windows due to open at 10 o'clock, as many as six thousand Beatles fans formed two long lines starting at the Gardens' two main entrances on Carlton Street. One stretched west for a block before bending north on Yonge Street. The other went east a few hundred feet and then up Church Street. About two dozen police kept order on the sidewalks.

So great was the crush forward at the stroke of ten that it

24

RIGHT:
Smelling a photo opportunity, Gardens executives Harold Ballard (front) and Stafford Smythe donned Beatle wigs and greeted the crowd gathered outside the arena.

BELOW:
Neither rain nor cold temperatures could deter Toronto fans.

took four cops and two Gardens guards just to get the doors open. Six girls and one boy fainted during that first mighty push. At the head of the line, surrounded by photographers, stood an exhausted Robin Timmerman, described as "bleary-eyed and shivering" in one press account. "I'm first and I'm proud of it," she exulted.

Not far behind Robin in the swell around the wickets were fifteen-year-old twins Edith and Herta Manea, famous among schoolmates as the Beatle-Manea sisters for the depths of their devotion to the Fab Four. They had taken turns skipping classes at St. Joseph's, a private girls' school, to keep their place in line.

"We desperately wanted tickets to that concert," Edith remembers. "By the time the Beatles played 'The Ed Sullivan Show' we were both madly in love. Crazed. Completely immersed in Beatlemania. Our parents were at their wits' end."

Photographers and reporters quickly zeroed in on the striking-looking twins, dressed in their school uniforms for a hasty return to classes that afternoon. "They asked us to scream and wave our tickets. Wow! That afternoon our pictures were on the front page of one of the papers. We were made with

ABOVE:
Beatle-Manea twins Herta and Edith (left and centre) with fellow Beatlemaniac Wanda Taylor during the height of Flower Power. The twins schemed for months to put Operation Beatles into effect.

LEFT:
CHUM DJ Bob McAdorey and fan club president Trudy Medcalf go on-air outside Maple Leaf Gardens.

FLASHBACK TO '64...
February 9 — Russia defeats Canada 3-2 to win the Olympic hockey gold medal; Canada finishes fourth.

all our friends."

But the nuns who ran St. Joseph's also saw the front page. "Beatlemania was something beyond their powers to understand," says Edith. "They pulled us from class and gave us a stern talking-to. Then they segregated us from the rest of the school. They even had us examined by a school psychologist. Finally, they suspended us for two weeks."

None of it mattered. "We had our tickets," Edith says. "What did any kind of punishment amount to compared to the importance of that?" She and Herta spent their two-week suspension carefully plotting their next moves in Operation Beatles. For the desperately infatuated Beatle-Manea twins, merely seeing their heroes perform would not be enough. They had to meet them, maybe even touch them. Nothing less, they agreed, would do.

In just one hour and fifteen minutes all available tickets sold out and the ticket windows slammed shut. That left four thousand or so bitterly disappointed adolescents standing outside in the rain, shouting in unison: "We want in!"

Of the 14,500 tickets printed for the show, close to seventy-five hundred had been set aside for ticket agencies and radio stations. Gardens management also

LEFT:
When the doors finally opened, six girls and one boy fainted in the crush.

29

held back several hundred of the choicest seats to meet the high demand from staff and VIPs. Approximately sixty-five hundred tickets remained for sale at the arena. Each buyer was limited to two apiece. Tickets cost from $4 to $5.50.

Even many near the front of the line came away disappointed with their purchases. All the ticket vendors could offer one teenage boy, who was only two hundred or so back in line, were seats well up the stands in the Greens. At least two thousand seats in the house afforded better views.

LEFT:
This elderly Beatlemaniac tried to push through the crowd and be first to the ticket window.

BELOW:
Flamboyant CHUM DJ Jungle Jay Nelson greets one of the first fans through the door.

31

"With so many kids unhappy with what they got, I felt even luckier to be first in the door," says Robin Timmerman. "There were so many reporters surrounding us that they had to give us good seats." But even she only made it into the third row. The seats in front of hers had been set aside in advance.

Outside the Gardens, the empty-handed thousands refused to budge, unable to accept that every last available ticket had been sold so quickly.

Then, after a wait of less than half an hour, the box office reopened. Tickets for a second show, a matinee, were put on sale, even though the Beatles had yet to agree to it. Stafford Smythe vowed to reporters that he would do whatever it took to secure the additional concert, including flying to England to meet with Beatles manager Brian Epstein.

That didn't prove necessary. Within weeks both Smythe and promoters in Montreal had successfully negotiated second shows. But the price was high. Epstein demanded a whopping seventy per cent of the gate, a full ten per cent more than for the evening concerts. (Contract terms with local promoters on the tour ranged from $20,000 to $40,000 per show, or sixty per cent of the total take, whichever was greater.)

By 1 p.m., three hours after the box office first opened, the line-ups on Carlton Street had disappeared, although some matinee tickets were still available.

HAVING MONITORED THE POTENTIALLY EXPLOSIVE SITUATION AT Maple Leaf Gardens, Montreal police proved far less accommodating than their Toronto counterparts when the first fans pitched camp outside the Forum's hallowed doors.

On May 14, the day before tickets went on sale, cops brusquely told about fifty girls who had gathered to either go home or sleep in Cabot Park, directly across from the Forum. But they worried needlessly. The sale the next day went off without a hitch.

West Coast Beatlemaniacs fretted until mid-June before confirmation finally came that there would indeed be a Vancouver concert — at Empire Stadium Saturday, August 22, opening night of the annual Pacific National Exhibition. The one-show stand, just the fourth stop of the tour, thus gave Vancouver the much-coveted honour of hosting B-Day, the history-making arrival of the Beatles in Canada.

PNE officials finally snagged the choice Saturday-night slot by being able to offer a stadium capable of seating twenty-seven thousand for a show of this type, double that of most other venues. The deal gave the Beatles their standard sixty per cent of the performance's gross revenue, forecast at $100,000.

Four days after the show had been confirmed, twenty-five hundred youngsters, a few of whom had slept out in the rain the previous two nights, formed ticket lines at the four corners of Empire Stadium. To avoid confusion or customer disappointment, staff stood ready at all sixteen of the stadium's permanent wickets. The sale started at 9:30. a.m. By

FAR LEFT:
Jubilant fan Sami Herbert smooches her hard-won tickets.

BELOW:
A newspaper ad for the Beatles' concert at Vancouver's Empire Stadium.

33

ADDITIONAL TICKETS AVAILABLE FOR

THE
BEATLES

at EMPIRE STADIUM
Aug. 22, 8:00 p.m.

Tickets on sale at: —
VANCOUVER
TICKET CENTRE
630 HAMILTON,
VANCOUVER
VICTORIA
— EATON'S BOX OFFICE
NANAIMO
— EATON'S BOX OFFICE
Admission Prices to show
and P.N.E.

$5.25 - 4.25 - 3.25

Prompt attention to Mall
Orders from Van. Ticket
Centre only.

Include stamped self-
addressed envelope with
cash or money-order.

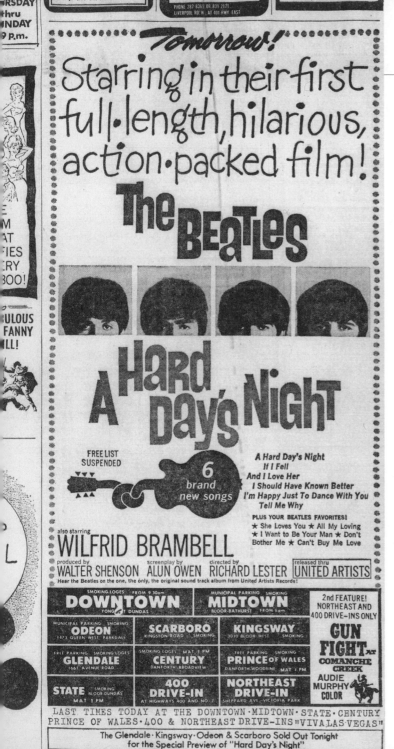

11 o'clock ten thousand tickets had been sold.

THE BEATLES CONTINUED TO COMMAND the world's attention all that spring and summer. Dozens of teenagers in Amsterdam jumped into the filthy canal water in an attempt to reach them when they toured the city by barge. During a visit to Australia, three hundred thousand fans lined the streets of Adelaide in welcome. To their credit, even the Beatles found this level of adulation ludicrous. The crowds reminded John Lennon of old newsreels he had seen of Hitler Youth rallies. Looking out over the multitudes from the balcony of their hotel, he placed a black comb under his nose to parody Hitler's moustache and led the lads in a snappy *Sieg Heil!*

Everything they touched turned to gold. John released *In His Own Write*, a slim book filled with his doodles, short essays and decidedly sophomoric puns. Naturally, it shot right to the top of the best-seller lists. Asked by a reporter if he made conscious use of the onomatopoeia, John looked puzzled. "Automatic pier? I don't know what you're going on about, son."

August saw the North American premiere of the Beatles' first feature film, *A

Hard Day's Night, yet another public triumph. Produced at a modest cost of $750,000 and directed by Richard Lester, the movie engagingly depicts thirty-six madcap hours in the life of the band. *"A Hard Day's Night*…is a bright and breezy entertainment," enthused the *Toronto Daily Star*. "Marx Brothers, move over. The Beatles…are witty in their own slapstick, Merseyside way," raved *The Gazette* in Montreal. American critic Andrew Sarris has since christened the film "The Citizen Kane of juke-box movies."

ABOVE:
By early 1964, Beatlemania had become a world-wide phenomenon. Here German girls hungrily eye an assortment of iced Beatle cakes.

FAR LEFT:
A newspaper ad for the Beatles' first film, A Hard Day's Night.

Only the Beatles themselves were less than thrilled with the final result. They felt that Wilfrid Brambell's brilliant comic turn in the role of Paul's grandfather, "the clean old man," stole the picture. They also insisted that scriptwriter Alun Owen failed to capture their personalities in anything but the most superficial way. The Beatles, who prided themselves on their rapier wit, agreed that they really were much funnier in real life than in the film.

Young girls began lining up at dawn when the movie opened in Canada. Once inside they charged straight to the front row, considered choice seats because of the extra swooning room. Les Wedman of the Vancouver *Sun* reluctantly attended the preview screening at the local Vogue theatre. "Don't ask me whether it's a good movie or a bad one!" he harrumphed. "I walked out of it less than twenty minutes after it started this morning – not because I wanted to, but because I

New Products of 1964 — Kellogg's Pop Tarts; Maxim, the first freeze-dried coffee; lift-top pop cans; G.I. Joe dolls; Japan's bullet train (designed to average 100 mph); the Ford Mustang.

had to before my eardrums split."

Even though the theatre's manager cranked the volume way up, only brief snippets of dialogue could be heard through the sobbing and wailing of the audience. "I've never seen anything like it in my life," the manager said, "and I've been in this business for twenty-five years."

Many fans, especially love-struck young females, saw *A Hard Day's Night* ten, fifteen and sometimes twenty or more times.

Just watching a short promotional clip from the movie was enough to turn one Montrealer, Eric Twiname, from a Beatle-hater into an instant convert. "I was fourteen at the time and a huge Buddy Holly fan," he remembers. "I felt it would be like committing adultery on Buddy to like the Beatles or anyone else. I'd even managed to make it through their appearances on

36

RIGHT:
Eager fans arrive early for a screening of A Hard Day's Night *at a Toronto theatre.*

BELOW:
Fan club president Trudy Medcalf's pass to a preview screening.

SPECIAL PREVIEW • ADMIT ONE
Tues. Aug. 11th at 8.30 p.m.
THE BEATLES
in their First Feature-Length Motion Picture
"A HARD DAY'S NIGHT"
Produced by Walter Shenson/Released Thru United Artists
ALL SEATS $1.00
THIS TICKET IS GOOD ONLY AT THE
KINGSWAY
THEATRE
3030 BLOOR ST. WEST

DO NOT DETACH, Present Entire Ticket To Doorman

'Ed Sullivan' without caving in. But then I saw a clip from the film of the Beatles singing 'I Should Have Known Better.' Game over. Resistance was futile. From that moment on I was a confirmed Beatles addict. I still am."

VANCOUVERITES GREW ALMOST MANIC WITH ANTICIPATION AS the hours counted down to the concert on August 22. Newspaper columnists vied with one another to see how many Beatles rumours they could successfully float, the more bizarre the better. One radio station offered to buy the beds the Beatles would sleep on during their overnight stay at the Hotel Georgia. With considerable fanfare, Eaton's opened a "Beatle Bar" on the main floor of its downtown store. The bar's inventory of "authentic" treasures included fourteen-inch Beatle combs, Beatle cushions, Beatle T-shirts, Beatle sneakers and Beatle hats decorated with four illustrations, but in one size only.

Police girded for the coming onslaught. At Empire Stadium, they oversaw the construction of four four-foot-high crush barriers, nicknamed Beatle Baffles, to separate the fans from the stage. A complement of two hundred constables would guard the various approaches. Extra PNE ushers and security guards were hired to patrol the stands.

According to the latest information received by Vancouver police, the Beatles planned to arrive in the early hours of Saturday by chartered jet from Seattle,

LEFT:
Paul McCartney and Wilfrid Brambell ("the clean old man") in a scene from A Hard Day's Night.

BELOW:
Vancouver's Hotel Georgia was tranformed into a veritable fortress in anticipation of the Beatles' arrival.

where they were to perform Friday night. A motorcycle squad would then escort them via an undisclosed route downtown to the Hotel Georgia. The luxurious Lord Stanley and Lord Nelson suites on the twelfth floor had been reserved for the Beatles' party. Police said they did not expect that the four would leave the hotel until just before showtime that evening. Afterwards, the Beatles would proceed directly back to the airport and then fly on to Los Angeles for a concert the next night at the Hollywood Bowl.

Work was feverishly under way to make the Georgia, as someone said, as impregnable as the Rock of Gibraltar. Workmen strung barbed wire around the building's perimeter. Plywood barricades covered all but the front door. Teams of Pinkerton security men would guard the elevators, stairs and fire escape.

Police felt they had done almost everything they could to prepare. But Peter Hudson, the Georgia's manager, lay awake nights haunted by visions of berserk adolescents pummelling down his front door and rampaging through the halls of his beautiful hotel. There had to be more they could do to secure the property. He made the decision that no one under twenty-one would be admitted to the hotel during the Beatles' stay unless accompanied by an adult. That at least would keep out teenage infiltrators bent on creating havoc.

And would it be possible, he wondered, to fly the Beatles by helicopter from the airport to the roof of the Georgia? That would avoid the possibility of a riot in the streets when the limousines carrying the band first arrived. Police thought the idea had merit, but the proposal was quickly rejected by the Ministry of Transport.

Soon people started joking that Hudson was the most nervous man in town. Almost at the last minute he placed a call to the manager of the hotel in Melbourne where the Beatles had stayed during their Australian tour. What advice did he have about how to handle their fans?

"I was given some useful tips," Hudson said afterward, "but I'm not saying what they were, because that would give the game away."

B-Day loomed.

B-Day Chapter 2

Winnipeg Free Press

ADVANCE TV CENTRE 636 SARGENT (NEAR SHERBROOK) PH. 786-33

WEDNESDAY, AUGUST 19, 1964

By Carrier 40c Per Week

Authorized as 2nd class mail by the P.O. Dept., Ottawa, and for payment of postage in cash.

DESPITE THE ELABORATE preparations of the Hotel Georgia's skittish manager and Vancouver police, in the end the Beatles' initial touchdown on Canadian soil managed to take almost everyone by surprise.

B–Day came not on the West Coast, but on a sun-baked prairie runway at Winnipeg International Airport. While en route from England to San Francisco for the opening tour date, the Beatles' chartered Lockheed Electra (designated Jet Clipper Beatles) dropped into Winnipeg for an unannounced refuelling stop that sent thousands of frantic fans racing to the airport by car, bus and on foot.

The Beatles left London for North America at noon on August 18. At that point only a handful of officials at Winnipeg International knew of the impending refuelling stop, scheduled

PRECEDING PAGES:
Police and stadium officials hold back ecstatic fans during the concert at Vancouver's Empire Stadium.

for about 2:05 p.m. local time and expected to last about twenty-five minutes. One of the first outsiders let in on the secret was Bob Burns, the twenty-six-year-old host of a popular teen dance show on local CJAY-TV (today's CKY-TV).

"Around noon I got a call from the public relations director for Air Canada in Winnipeg, who was a good friend of mine," Burns remembers. "'Get out to the airport for the interview of your life,' he told me. 'And make sure you keep this under your hat: The Beatles will be here in less than two hours.'

"I raced around the station until I finally found a cameraman who was free. Then we made a beeline for the airport. The Mounties on duty let me go right out onto the tarmac, where the plane would taxi in."

But if Burns hoped for a scoop, he was sorely disappointed. The few others in the know must have also been busy on the telephone. By the time he arrived, more than three hundred wailing youngsters lined the rails of the third-floor observation deck.

Around the same time at least two Winnipeg radio stations announced that the Beatles' plane would land at any moment. Immediately all roads leading to the airport became clogged with traffic. RCMP officers on duty at the terminal radioed for reinforcements as several hundred more fans arrived almost simultaneously.

Some escaped the congestion on the observation deck by climbing out onto the concrete roof of the terminal; others tried to sneak their way back down the stairs to join airport technicians and other personnel who had abandoned their posts and pushed out onto the runway

The Beatles' unannounced stop at Winnipeg International sent hundreds of teenagers racing to the airport to catch a glimpse of their idols.

45

apron for a better look. By now the size of the Beatles' reception was estimated at more than one thousand.

Feeding the frenzy was the total shock of the Beatles' arrival in Winnipeg. What started as just another hot and lazy summer afternoon had suddenly offered local Beatlemaniacs a momentous opportunity. This, they knew, was likely their one chance to see the Fab Four in the flesh.

By 2 p.m. all pretence of secrecy had been abandoned by airport officials. A deafening scream erupted when a voice over the public-address system intoned: "Pan American announces the arrival of the Beatle special from London…."

Lusty choruses of "We want the Beatles!" greeted the plane as it taxied in. While medical personnel checked the passengers' health, the crowd waited impatiently for their heroes to appear.

RIGHT:
"Hello Winnipeg!" Though reluctant at first to come out of their airplane during the brief refuelling stop, the Beatles soon warmed to their task.

BELOW:
CJAY-TV's Bob Burns reports from the tarmac of Winnipeg International. Thanks to a tip from an airport official, Burns became the first person ever to interview the band in Canada.

"What people didn't realize was that the Beatles had absolutely no intention of coming out of their airplane," Bob Burns says. "I was told that Brian Epstein had to work hard to convince them. Maybe they were exhausted after the long flight. But Epstein knew that it would have been a public-relations disaster to disappoint so many kids – especially right at the start of the tour."

Soon the Beatles appeared at the airplane door and waved energetically in the direction of the deck. Still waving, they made their way down the stairs towards Burns and his cameraman, several newspapermen and a crew from a rival TV station.

But they talked to Burns first. "I get a real kick out of that, being the first person ever to interview

ABOVE LEFT AND RIGHT:
Winnipeg teen Bruce Decker dashes up the ramp to the plane carrying the Beatles. Newswire photos of his bare-footed run for glory were reprinted around the world.

them in Canada," he says. "It's fun being a little piece of history."

Unfortunately, neither Burns nor any of the others got much from the Beatles. They seemed almost manic after being cooped up in their airplane during the long flight.

"Wah, wah, wah," John Lennon responded to one query, breaking into a frenzied dance. "You must be glad to stretch your legs," Burns said to him. "Amongst other things, yes," John replied.

"I found him a bit of a scallywag," Burns says. "He had a smart-aleck answer for everything I asked."

Paul McCartney was better. "It's a luverly welcome," he said. "And it was a beautiful flight."

George Harrison's head seemed still in a London fog.

Asked about upcoming tour dates, he replied that he had no idea of the band's itinerary beyond the opening concert. "We don't know where we're going after San Francisco…. We never know where we're going."

The only Beatle who treated any of the questions seriously was Ringo Starr. He announced that the group's next movie would be in theatres by the following February. "He seemed more mature than the others," recalls Burns, who would meet up with the band again the next month in Toronto. "Ringo appeared to be handling their sudden fame like more of an adult."

After about ten minutes, their duty done, the four climbed back up the stairs to a deafening serenade of "We want the Beatles." A reporter observed that by this point the noise from the observation deck had reached "hysteria level." With a final flurry of waves, the Beatles disappeared inside the Electra.

It was at exactly this moment – after the refuelling crews had finished their work but before the door of the airplane closed – that Bruce Decker, a burly seventeen-year-old on the football squad at Silver Heights Collegiate, saw an opening in the Beatles' defence and made a barefooted run for glory captured in a series of wire-service photos reprinted around the world.

Wearing only a striped shirt and cut-off shorts, Decker was on his way to the beach with friends when they heard about the Beatles' arrival on the car radio. "We decided to head

ABOVE:
The Mounties get their man.

49

FLASHBACK TO '64…
February 25 — Cassius Clay (the future Muhammad Ali) wins the world heavyweight boxing crown with a seventh-round TKO of Sonny Liston at Miami Beach.

for the airport," he said, "and by the time we got there, the Beatles had already gone into the plane."

Decker and his pals were among those who managed to sneak down from the observation deck onto the tarmac. "There was a group of girls standing near me and they were saying how they'd like to storm the stairs of the plane." He thought that if he got a foot in the airplane's door, he'd be able to at least see the Beatles and that they might even talk to him.

Decker's twenty-five-yard dash across the tarmac and up the stairs ended abruptly when he collided with a startled Pan American airport manager, who was just coming out of the cabin. A trio of Mounties scrambled up the stairs and completed the tackle.

"Just as they were wrestling with me, I caught a glimpse of the Beatles through the door and they were all chuckling," Decker said. "I just did it for a bit of fun and didn't realize there was anything serious attached to it."

Following a stern warning, the Mounties set him free to enjoy his moment of fame. "After the police had let me go, a girl recognized me and begged me to let her take my photo. Then another two girls saw me and pushed me into a corner. Tears were streaming down their faces as they asked me: 'What did they look like? Did they say anything? How does Ringo look?'"

So unexpected, the Beatles' brief visit to Winnipeg made a spectacular impact. "We've never seen anything like this before – and I hope we won't see it again," said Sgt. E. G. Varndell, RCMP chief at Winnipeg International.

Dozens of young girls lingered on at the airport after the Beatles departed, sobbing and wandering about in a daze. A police car was dispatched to the tarmac, where a crowd of about thirty was kissing the spot where the airplane had sat. Other girls planted kisses on the stairs where the boys had stood dur-

The Beatles opened their North American tour with a concert at San Francisco's Cow Palace. One local reporter compared the din to "a jet engine shrieking through a summer lightning storm."

ing the impromptu press conference. Out near the carpark, still others were crying and rolling around on the grass.

It took Sgt. Varndell's men until about 4:15 p.m., almost two hours after Jet Clipper Beatles had vanished on the horizon, to finally clear the airport.

FOLLOWING A BRIEF STOP IN LOS ANGELES, THE ELECTRA landed to a tumultuous welcome from nine thousand fans at San Francisco International Airport. The moment the Beatles stepped from the airplane, the crowd surged forward, toppling a fence and stampeding across the tarmac.

Visibly shaken, the Beatles just narrowly escaped by limousine to the safety of their heavily guarded fifteenth-floor suite at the Hilton. That evening, in the streets below, about two thousand fans produced such a constant clamour that the

FLASHBACK TO '64...
March 10 — Queen Elizabeth gives birth to her fourth child, Edward.

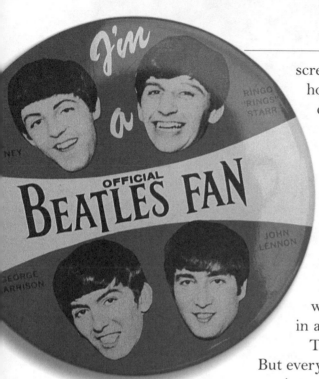

Buttons like this one in mint condition now cost about $15.

screams of a woman being robbed and beaten on the hotel's sixth floor went unheeded. A maid mistook her cries for the shrieks coming from outside.

The Beatles gave their first concert of the tour the next night at San Francisco's Cow Palace. "Although it was publicized as music, all that was heard and seen of the Mersey Sound was something like a jet engine shrieking through a summer lightning storm because of the yelling fans," reported the *San Francisco Examiner*. After the show, when their driver hesitated a moment in pulling away, the Beatles' limo was overrun and nearly crushed by the weight of fans before security forces managed to move in and pull them to safety.

The Beatles had long grown accustomed to the insanity. But everything they encountered in America struck them as scarier and somehow darker than anything they had experienced before. In a country that had a history of killing its presidents, what was to prevent some madman from claiming his Beatle? "We sometimes wondered after we stepped off the plane," Ringo Starr recalled, "if we'd walk to Customs or be carried…*Bang!*"

"It was terrifying and terrific all at once," the drummer said on another occasion. "Some nights I just sat there behind my drums and stared out across the sea of faces in front of the stage or the platform. It's the sheer size of everything in America that's frightening. But I must say that doing a show for such a huge audience gives you a marvellous buzz. There are so many voices available out there to do the screaming that it's one continuous sound."

Everything in America was for sale, most of all Beatlemania. Several of the hotels they stayed at shamelessly auctioned off authenticated swatches of their unlaundered sheets, pillowcases and towels. In New York City, the capital of greed, an entrepreneur marketed empty cans of what he called "Beatle Breath."

During the Beatles' stay at the San Francisco Hilton, Brian Epstein received a visit from Charles O. Finley, the flamboyant owner of the Kansas City Athletics baseball club. Despite previous overtures, Kansas City had been excluded from the already crowded tour schedule. But Finley had gone out on a limb and personally promised his fellow Kansans that he would deliver the Beatles.

Finley opened the negotiations by offering Epstein a guaranteed $100,000 in cash, a staggering figure at the time.

Epstein's answer was still no. The boys had too few off-days as it was and would need their rest.

A week later, Finley broke down Epstein's resistance with an offer of $150,000 plus expenses, which worked out to roughly $4,838 for every minute the Beatles would occupy the stage. No act in history had ever been paid anything close to that amount. Barbra Streisand had set the previous high of $35,050 with a concert at the Hollywood Bowl. The Beatles, Epstein sensibly concluded, could rest up when they got back home to England.

The biggest act in entertainment history rolled towards Vancouver, the fourth stop on the tour. The Beatles performed two shows at the Las Vegas Convention Center on August 20. After someone called in a bomb threat, they gamely went on for the second concert knowing that every Beatle breath they took might be their last.

A riot erupted later that night when they were delivered back to the Sahara Hotel. Things got even further out of hand the next evening in Seattle, where a girl who had climbed out

53

FLASHBACK TO '64...
March 13 — Parliament approves a plan to send 1,150 Canadian troops to Cyprus as part of a UN peace-keeping force.

onto a beam over the stage fell in a clump in front of Ringo's drum set. At concert's end, police called upon navy volunteers from the audience to help form a human barricade from the stage to the dressing room. The Beatles stayed trapped in the building for almost an hour.

Vancouver police grew ever more apprehensive as the news reports came in. Headquarters dispatched Superintendent Ben Jelley to the Seattle-Tacoma airport to study the crowd reaction and police strategy when the Beatles landed. Jelley's report of the typically unrestrained reception there convinced his superiors to have the Beatles' plane land at the RCAF base adjacent to Vancouver International Airport. There the band could be assured virtually airtight security.

There was another last-minute change in plans: Brian Epstein decided that the band would sleep over in Seattle on Friday night rather than fly on to Vancouver, as originally planned. They were now expected to arrive sometime early Saturday afternoon. From the RCAF base the Beatles would proceed directly to the Hotel Georgia, where they'd rest in their suites and then conduct a press conference before heading to Empire Stadium.

AUGUST 22, CONCERT DAY, DAWNED FAIR AND MILD IN VANCOUVER. Outside the Georgia, fans had been gathering since before first light. Mostly they were girls between the ages of ten and fourteen. Some scribbled their names in lipstick on the plywood barricades that blocked all but the hotel's front door. Inside, safe for the moment in a washroom storage closet, huddled a trio of girls who for the past three days had managed to elude the security sweeps of Pinkertons hired by hotel manager Peter Hudson.

With the racket going on all around, Dr. Lou Beckstead

and his family had gotten very little sleep that night in their suite at the Georgia. Dr. Beckstead, a Winnipeg internist, his wife, Veta, and their two children, nineteen-year-old Jim and ten-year-old Sharon, were supposed to be enjoying a quiet family vacation on the Coast. If the doctor, who always got a little cranky when deprived of his sleep, had known they'd have to share the hotel with the Beatles, he would never have made the reservation in the first place.

None too surprisingly, his children held exactly the opposite opinion. "You could have scraped me off the ceiling when we arrived on Friday night and found out the Georgia would be the Beatles' hotel," Sharon remembers. "I was an absolute Beatle fanatic. Forget the noise outside; I was so excited I wouldn't have gotten a wink of sleep that night anyway."

"It was just this incredible stroke of good fortune," agrees Jim, then a pre-med student at the University of Manitoba. "To land like that in the middle of the biggest story in Canada. What are the odds?"

Just as big a surprise was the discovery that their straight-arrow father had phoned ahead and booked four tickets to the Beatles' concert at Empire Stadium. "Jim and I were both literally in shock," laughs Sharon. "My nickname for our father was Straight-Laced Lou. He was a man who preferred opera and the symphony. Buying those tickets was so out of character that you just had to love him for it."

Typically, a Beckstead family vacation included obligatory visits to local museums, galleries and other dreary cultural outposts that Sharon and Jim would have given almost anything to avoid. And that was pretty much the itinerary planned for that day. But Jim was having none of it. He defiantly told his angry father that he intended to wait at the hotel for the arrival of the Beatles. "It was just too big an opportunity to pass up," he says.

Veta, Sharon and Jim Beckstead, whose family vacation in Vancouver unexpectedly plunged them into the full frenzy of Beatlemania.

55

Though she stormed and pouted, Sharon lost her battle to stay behind with her big brother. "I'm sure I was impossible all day and they probably wished they had left me at the hotel. My only consolation was I knew I'd be seeing the Beatles that night."

By mid-afternoon the crowd outside the Hotel Georgia had swelled to about four thousand. Some of them had been there for as long as thirteen hours. Oblivious to the cuts and scrapes on their legs, three desperate girls attempted to scale the Georgia's fire escape, which the Pinkertons had decorated with barbed wire.

Red Robinson, one of the city's most popular disc jockeys as well as the program director at C-FUN, the top-rated AM station in Vancouver, carefully monitored the situation outside the Georgia all that day. The twenty-six-year-old was largely responsible for introducing West Coast teens to rock 'n' roll back in the mid-1950s. In 1957, he acted as master of ceremonies for Elvis Presley's only local appearance, an evening one newspaper called "the most disgusting exhibition of mass hysteria this city has ever seen." Tonight, he would have the honour of hosting the Beatles' concert.

Natural flamboyance and an unerring sense of showmanship were the cornerstones of Robinson's success. The flame-haired DJ had an uncanny gift for whipping young audiences into a frenzy. Now, at a point when all his instincts told him the crowd outside the Georgia had reached its peak, Robinson launched what he considered the greatest promotional stunt of his career.

First, he put rumours out on the air that Ringo Starr had been seen driving around the city. Then a station employee, a young fellow who already bore a striking resemblance to the

Red Robinson (centre left), who acted as master of ceremonies for the Beatles' concert, along with the rest of the on-air crew at Vancouver's C-FUN-AM. The Fab Four's appearance inspired Robinson to hatch the most outrageous publicity stunt of his colourful career.

Elvis and the Four Kings

OF ALL ROCK 'N' ROLL entertainers, only Elvis Presley has ever approached the popularity of the Beatles. Three times in 1957, during the first flush of his fame, Presley played to adoring Canadian audiences — in Vancouver, Ottawa and Toronto. They were the only appearances the King would ever make outside the United States.

At Empire Stadium in Vancouver, Elvis, wearing his trademark gold lamé jacket, rode onto the field in a black Cadillac convertible. "The crowd went berserk," remembers radio personality Red Robinson, who hosted that show as well as the Beatles' concert seven years later. "It sounded like a city of a million all screaming and yelling in unison."

John, Paul, George and Ringo worshipped Elvis. Early on they had honed their skills playing such Presley hits as "Hound Dog" and "That's All Right (Mama)." The boys had long hoped to meet their idol and pay their respects.

During the Beatles' 1965 North American tour, a summit conference was arranged at Presley's home in Los Angeles. Elvis was ensconced on the sofa, surrounded by his coterie of sycophants, the Memphis Mafia. In the background, a jukebox played an alternating selection of Fab Four and Presley hits.

For the first five minutes, the Beatles, awed to finally be in his presence, sat and gazed at Elvis, barely saying a word. "Look, if you damn guys are gonna sit and stare at me all night,"

Presley finally burst out, "I'm gonna go to bed."

Things improved only slightly after that. They listened to the music and discussed the difficulties of living with the type of fame that so far only the five of them had ever achieved. John Lennon said later that he went away from the meeting disappointed and slightly depressed. Elvis, obviously stoned, had seemed out of it and maybe even a little, well, thick.

Some who knew the King said the real problem was that he felt threatened by the Beatles. By that point in his career the number-one hits were few and far between for Elvis and he had been reduced to starring in B-movie stinkers like *Blue Hawaii* and *Girls! Girls! Girls!* In the Beatles' success, Presley saw the proof of his own eclipse.

Red Robinson with Elvis Presley in 1957.

Beatles' drummer, was outfitted with sunglasses and a wig and sent out towards the Georgia in a shiny red convertible.

One reporter likened it to pouring "gasoline on troubled waters." As the car approached the hotel, someone screamed, "There's Ringo!" Within seconds the convertible was engulfed by hundreds of screeching girls. Police had to fight their way through the mob to rescue the terrified impersonator and his driver.

"I took a lot of heat for that stunt – and rightly so," Robinson says today. "It was a hare-brained idea that could have gotten people hurt. But, of course, I didn't think of that at the time. It just seemed like a funny gag."

AT THE RCAF SIDE OF THE AIRPORT, SECURITY PATROLS TURNED away hundreds of fans who attempted to defy a day-long ban on unofficial visitors. Only one hundred and fifty people – mostly the families of air force and Royal Canadian Mounted Police officers, air cadets and other air force personnel – waited to welcome the Beatles to Vancouver.

After taking off from Seattle, the Electra was ordered back to the airport to complete the pilot's customs clearance (John Lennon later wisecracked that, in fact, they had all needed delousing). The Beatles finally landed in Vancouver late in the afternoon, leaving no time for a rest stop at the Hotel Georgia. Brian Epstein decided that the motorcade would instead take a forty-minute Cook's tour of the city, ending at Empire Stadium about 7 p.m. The planned press conference would have to be squeezed in before the start of the show.

Police outside the Georgia gladly announced the change in plans, shuddering to think what might have happened if the real Ringo and his partners had arrived. At first there were howls of outrage at the news. But the crowd quickly dispersed without incident. For those with concert tickets, it was almost time to head for the stadium.

Jim Beckstead, the pre-med student on vacation with his family, remembers that staff and guests inside the hotel didn't quite know what to believe. Maybe this was all some sort of security diversion. Jim felt miffed at wasting an entire day of his holiday, but like his little sister he consoled himself by looking ahead to the show that night.

Peter Hudson, the careworn manager of the Hotel Georgia, can only have heaved a tremendous sigh of relief, especially after word came that Brian Epstein had agreed to pay the $350 bill for the luxury suites the Beatles never used.

Through the darkened windows of their limousine, John,

59

Taken by teenager Jim Beckstead, this photo shows the growing crowd outside Vancouver's Hotel Georgia before the Beatles' anticipated arrival.

Paul, George and Ringo viewed beautiful Vancouver with eyes jaded by a hundred similar tours in a hundred different cities. Vancouver was no different than anyplace else they'd seen, quipped one Beatle, it has trees. After a pit stop at a roadside diner for a take-out order of nineteen-cent hamburgers and chicken wings, their motorcade was met by an ear-piercing shriek from onlookers as it entered the Pacific National Exhibition fair grounds and proceeded on to Empire Stadium.

THIRTY-TWO SHOWS IN THIRTY-FOUR DAYS IN TWENTY-FOUR cities – and at every stop during the 1964 North American tour legions of Beatlemaniacs attempted to outscream and outsob and in every other way demonstrate a devotion surpassing that shown in every city that had come before.

Beatlemania swept up fans of all ages, including children still colouring with crayons.

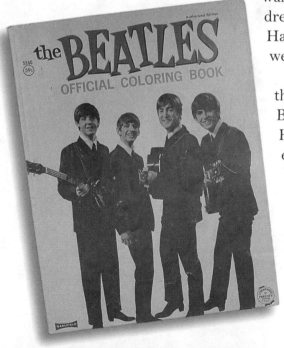

The Beatles were prisoners in a gilded cage, unable to wander more than a few feet from their hotel suite or dressing room. It really wasn't so bad, said George Harrison, "so long as we have our ciggies and corn flakes we don't mind being cooped up."

Still, the pent-up restlessness and the demands on their patience sometimes became intolerable. After the Beatles had moved on from Vancouver to Hollywood, Harrison poured a drink over the head of a photographer. "We were invited down to the Café Whisky à Go Go by the manager and this nasty little photographer kept leaping in snapping pictures, so I finally blessed him," George explained. "He was an uncouth youth."

Later in the tour, an executive with a girdle-manufacturing firm grabbed hold of Paul McCartney's coat and refused to let go. Blows were exchanged over that episode.

"Would you like to walk down the street without

being recognized?" a reporter asked John Lennon when they landed in North America the first time. "We used to do that with no money in our pockets," he answered. "There's no point in it." But while in Las Vegas, Lennon stared wistfully up at the blacked-out penthouse apartment of billionaire Howard Hughes, the world's most famous recluse. "That would suit me fine," he said. "In one place forever instead of this constant travelling. Total privacy. Nobody to bother you."

On August 27, while the Beatles were on stage in Cincinnati playing in 115-degree heat, thieves stole cash and personal items from their dressing room.

The four were also badly rattled when an astrologer made headlines with the prediction that the Beatles' chartered airplane would crash sometime during the tour. She was nearly right: the Electra did go down – but not until April 1966, when it crashed with eighty soldiers on board.

Following their show in Atlantic City on August 30, the Beatles looked forward to a two-day break in New York. But the pandemonium in the streets outside the Delmonico Hotel squashed any thoughts of their leaving the suite. Horses of the NYPD's mounted division, specially trained to stay calm in crowds, had to be given quiet breaks after just ten minutes on the barricades. The tension inside the Beatles' suite was described as electric.

Word from Indianapolis on September 3 that John Lennon and George Harrison had developed sore throats stopped thou-

At every stop on the tour, Beatlemaniacs strove to demonstrate a devotion surpassing that shown in every other city. Here high school student Myra Lowenthal puts the last loving touches on a portrait of John Lennon before the band's appearance in Toronto.

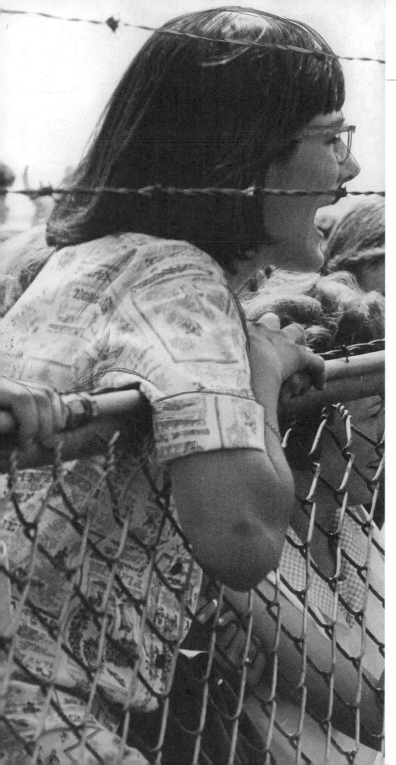

sands of young Canadian hearts. For a day or two speculation abounded that the concerts in Toronto and Montreal on the seventh and eighth would have to be cancelled. All four Beatles were fighting exhaustion by the time they finished their second of two shows in Detroit the night of September 6 and boarded the Electra for the short hop to Toronto.

FULLY TEN THOUSAND FANS, ONE OF THE largest receptions of the entire tour, stood ready to restore the Beatles with the power of their love early that holiday Monday morning at Toronto International Airport.

They began arriving about 11:30 p.m. on Saturday, staking positions behind a barbed-wire-topped chain-link fence out by the hangar-like firehall, which was to act as an impromptu customs office for the Beatles' arrival. Twenty-four hours later the crowd had grown almost to its limit, illuminated by the glare of television lights and stretching back into the darkness for more than a thousand feet along the main road leading into the airport. Some three hundred RCMP, Ontario Provincial Police and Metro Toronto Police constables stood on guard behind the fence and patrolled the airport grounds.

Beside the firehall, limousines and the motorcycles of a police escort awaited the

Beatles' journey downtown to the King Edward Hotel, their home that night and the next. With the earlier change of plans in Vancouver, Toronto would now be the only Canadian city to wake up with the Beatles. Epstein intended to fly them in and out of Montreal the same day.

The crowd seethed and shoved and laughed together as 12:15 a.m., the Electra's estimated time of arrival, drew near. Some waved their crudely made signs of welcome for the TV cameras. Occasionally, a girl would start screaming, and then another would pick up on it and still more would join in. And they sang – every Beatles hit from "Love Me Do" to "A Hard Day's Night," the latest chart-topper. But by far the most popular tune was "O-Beatles," an improvisation of "O Canada."

By midnight, at least two thousand of the ten thousand on hand were uncomfortably squeezed together behind the two-hundred-foot length of the firehall fence. As latecomers in the rear tried to push forward for a better look, young girls at the front, some as young as ten, began sobbing for help. Barbed wire dug into the throat of one and tore the sweater of another. Police carried girls who had fainted into the waiting arms of St. John Ambulance crews. Television cameramen, attempting to move in to film the scene, added to the confusion.

Doubled over as if in pain, a fourteen-year-old girl who lost her prime vantage point in escaping the crush wailed, "I wanted to see Ringo and now I've given up. Can you believe that I've actually given up? I've been here since 10 o'clock this morning and now these people have come and pushed me out. These people, they're terrible. Ringo would hate them. I know he would."

The squeal of welcome that greeted the Beatles' landing all but drowned out the growl of the Electra's engines. Then everyone held his or her breath and waited. For fifteen

FAR LEFT:
One of largest and wildest receptions of the entire tour awaited the Beatles at Toronto International Airport. Here a frantic girl clings to the barbed-wire-topped fence at the tarmac's edge.

63

FLASHBACK TO '64...
March 27 — The worst earthquake in U.S. history hits Anchorage, Alaska, flattening more than three-quarters of the city. The death toll reaches 118 throughout the state.

excruciating minutes they stood poised to scream their lungs out while Canadian customs agents entered the plane and put the occupants through the standard drill.

Having to deal with officials such as these was one of the Beatles' pet peeves. Almost all used their positions to insist on autographs before allowing anyone to disembark. Signing for fans was one thing, George Harrison complained to a Toronto reporter on the flight from Detroit, but "we don't like being asked for autographs by the officials. Everywhere we go it's always the police guarding us or the journalists or relatives of the promoters who ask us to sign."

Sure enough, first on board at Toronto International were two immigration nurses who walked directly to the back of the plane where the Beatles were sitting, gave the four a cursory glance, and then asked them to sign their autographs on triplicate form papers.

Sitting at the front of the cabin with all of the occupants' passports and other documentation piled on his lap, another immigration official said, "This we can look after later, let's have their autographs."

At last, Paul McCartney stuck his head out the door and into the glare of a thousand flash bulbs. An avid shutterbug who faithfully documented every stop on the tour, Paul flashed right back at them with his own camera.

As the Beatles emerged, the link fence alongside the tarmac bulged ominously. Fans climbed on top of one another, craning for a better look. Constables hastily reinforced the fence with plank props. Then they linked arms and formed a last line of defence in case it toppled.

After such a long build-up, the pay-off hardly seemed worth the wait. With barely a wave, the Beatles raced down the stairs, through the firehall, and into the lead car of a five-

LEFT:
By the time of the Beatles' arrival at Toronto International, at least two thousand of the ten thousand fans on hand were uncomfortably squeezed together behind a two-hundred-foot length of fence.

65

FLASHBACK TO '64...
April 1 — In an effort to ease bureaucratic record-keeping, Ottawa issues social insurance numbers to every employed Canadian.

66

OFFICIAL MEMBERSHIP CARD
BEATLES FAN CLUB

Name

Address

Paul McCartney   George Harrison

Ringo Starr

John Lennon

limousine convoy, which sped off almost instantly.

One observer estimated that the sprint from the door of the airplane to their limousine took no more than twenty-six seconds. None of the Beatles stood still long enough for any of the fans to get a good look.

"I don't remember actually seeing the Beatles at the airport," says Pat Sibley, who was right in front. Together with two friends she had met that April in the Beatles ticket line-up, Pat, then seventeen, had been the first to arrive at the airport Saturday night. "I must have seen them, but it all happened so fast, and with all the noise and confusion, I just don't remember."

Even the Beatles' route out of the airport proved a disappointment. The procession sped off along a dirt service road in a restricted area and on out of the airport towards downtown by a back road. Yet all through the day police had told new arrivals that the Beatles would definitely take the main road out of the airport. Unable to get anywhere close to the front near the firehall, most of the ten thousand on hand positioned themselves along this route.

The general consensus was that no more than five hundred lucky fans – some put the actual number at closer to fifty – caught even a glimpse of the Beatles at the airport. Of those, as one reporter noted, "many finished the night with bruises, barbed-wire scratches and aching ribs after being crushed unmercifully into the fence."

Before the Beatles' arrival, an RCMP spokesman had said, "We, as well as the city and provincial forces, have promised to do all we can to let the kids get a look at the Beatles. Within the bounds of safety and common sense, we intend to stick

Edmonton

630 kc

August 18th, 1964

Dear Beatle Fan Parent:

This letter will serve as your official confirmation and per-
mission for your child to attend the Beatle concert in Vancouver
on the CHED "Beatle Blast". They must arrive at the Edmonton
International Airport at 3:00 P.M. Saturday with this letter.
Keith James, Station Program Director, should be presented with
this letter upon arrival.

The flight to Vancouver is approximately two hours and ten minutes, which means we will arrive there at approximately 6:00 P.M.
A meal will be served on the plane. The show is at Vancouver
Stadium at 8:00 P.M. and will run approximately until 10:00 P.M.,
at which time we will leave the stadium by chartered bus back to
the Vancouver airport. We plan to leave Vancouver at approximately 11:30 P.M., depending upon traffic conditions at the
stadium and in the city. The return flight will take approximately two hours and ten minutes, so we plan to arrive at about
1:30 A.M. at the Edmonton International Airport. Due to the
uncertainty of traffic conditions, we may be a little early or
a little late, but parents are asked to tune CHED Radio at around
midnight to hear the announcement of the exact arrival time.

We appreciate the parents' co-operation and instructing the
youngsters to respect the authority of the CHED personnel and
plane crew in keeping things orderly. We know they are
to have a good time, and hope it will be one of the
memorable and exciting experiences.

Sincerely,

RADIO STATION CHED

Keith James

Keith James
Program Director

KJ/dc

to this promise."

One of the few completely satisfied fans at the airport was seventeen-year-old Donna Smith of Toronto. She enjoyed the good fortune of having been squeezed into unconsciousness in the surge of excitement when the Electra landed. Handed over the fence, she got as close as anyone not in a uniform to the Beatles.

"I saw George and he looked at me and I saw John too. You know, it's not that I'm in love with them or anything," she insisted. "It's just that their music has *something....*"

RCMP AND LOCAL POLICE WOULD EVEN MORE RIGIDLY DEFINE the bounds of safety and common sense when the Beatles landed at Montreal International Airport some thirty-seven hours and two Toronto concerts later. They confined all fans to the second-storey observation gallery, a reassuring twenty-five feet above ground. Almost three hundred RCMP and local police were on duty for the landing in Dorval, several times the number assigned to even the most important diplomatic arrivals. St. John Ambulance had two hundred attendants on site. Police officials boasted that they could handle a crowd of twenty-seven thousand if necessary.

Paul McCartney had wondered aloud if the Beatles would be welcome in Montreal, what with them being British and the separatist movement gaining steadily in popularity throughout Quebec. In recent months, the FLQ (Quebec Liberation Front), separatism's militant wing, had captured headlines with a series of bombings and by issuing death threats against the Queen.

The most accurate answer to Paul's query was that Beatlemania transcended all political convictions – in Quebec as everywhere else. A reception of five thousand youngsters, many of them skipping off the first day of school to be there, waited in the rain to greet them Tuesday afternoon.

But, in fact, there were serious concerns about the Beatles' safety in Montreal. Someone had called police threatening to shoot Ringo Starr for being an English Jew. "I am English, but I'm not Jewish," protested Ringo, who admitted to being a nervous wreck throughout the band's short stay in the city.

The Beatles, who like all celebrities were used to dealing with the occasional lunatic, had received death threats before, yet never in such a politically charged atmosphere. Cancelling the shows wasn't an option. Too much money was at stake and

Singing Beatles songs in Canada's two official languages, a reception of five thousand fans greeted the Fab Four at Montreal International Airport.

none of the four wanted to disappoint their fans, who were never told of the threat against Ringo. "We'll not be anybody's pawns," said John Lennon stubbornly. "We're here to play music."

Considering the bad weather and the demands of academia, the turnout at Montreal International seemed entirely respectable; about the average for all cities on the tour. But compared to the massive welcome in Toronto, the presumably staid anglo bastion scorned by every Montrealer, it seemed not nearly enough.

Jody Fine, president of the local chapter of the Beatles fan club, felt obliged to try to explain away the gap. "Many are too young and their parents wouldn't let them go," she said of Montreal fans. "Besides, we were not sure they would land at Dorval." Because of the uncertainty, she had earlier advised fan club members not to show up at the airport.

The peculiar charm of this reception was the singing of Beatles tunes in two languages. Otherwise, there was the steady build-up of chants and shouts and spontaneous outbursts of screaming seen everywhere else. Every plane that approached the airport punched up the level of excitement.

Heavy rain had tapered off to a light drizzle by the time Jet Clipper Beatles put down at 2:24 p.m. The pilot of the Beatles' plane taxied to a point on the tarmac where everyone on the observation deck could get a good look.

Paul is smiling but Ringo appears to be peering nervously out at the crowd at the airport in Montreal. A death threat against the drummer was received by police before the Beatles' arrival.

First out again was Paul, camera at the ready. McCartney pretended to be surprised by the mob on the observation deck and faked a heart attack. But it was Ringo, flanked by two plain-clothes detectives, who got the biggest cheer. The Beatles stood smiling and waving first on the ramp and then on the ground for about thirty seconds before aides shoved them into their black limousine.

By now the drizzle had become a downpour. As the limousine sped off, soaked fans raced to the front of the airport for a last look.

The Beatles said later that the trip downtown to the Forum offered more excitement than they bargained for. Speeding ahead of the motorcycle escort, their chauffeur ran two red lights before a sharp rebuke from a shaken George Harrison finally slowed him down.

Assassination threats and berserk crowds the Beatles could handle, but their first experience of a Montreal driver was something else again.

A change purse dating from the heyday of Beatlemania.

71

Besieged **Chapter 3**

"I THOUGHT I WAS FOR IT," said Paul McCartney, displaying his torn shirt. "But an immense copper lifted me up and shoved me into the elevator."

Surrounded by aides and a privileged handful of reporters, the Beatles recounted their death-defying dash into Toronto's King Edward Hotel just minutes before.

"We got separated from John and George coming in but the police were very good," Ringo added.

"The best view of the country," quipped John, "is over the blue shoulder of a policeman."

More than a hundred constables, including a mounted squad, had ringed the downtown hotel. But at first they proved no match for the five thousand zealots who ambushed the Beatles' car when it pulled up at 1:06 Monday morning after the trip from the air-

PRECEDING PAGES:
John Lennon is seen at the centre of a shouting, pushing mob that ambushed the Beatles as they arrived at Toronto's King Edward Hotel.

port. Wave after wave tore into the police line until at last it crumbled. Fans swarmed the car like locusts.

For a breathless few moments, the Beatles were at the mercy of a mob that clearly had none. Hysterical teens clawed at the car's windows and door handles, trying to fight their way in.

Just barely in time, the police regrouped. Using their horses as shields, they formed a flying wedge that pushed the horde back from the limo. Then out the door popped Ringo, who shouted "Yahoo" and dashed for the King Edward's front door, his three partners on his heels. During their escape, someone reached out and tore a button from Paul's shirt.

The Beatles burst into a hotel lobby jammed with reporters, television crews, hotel staff and guests. Positioned by the elevators, Edith and Herta Manea, the fanatically devoted Beatle-Manea twins, stared wide-eyed at their idols' entrance. The two had plotted, schemed and even stolen to make this very moment a reality.

Operation Beatles, the culmination of their vow to make a personal connection with the Fab Four, had unfolded in three meticulously planned stages over the past months. Stage One had been the securing of complete access to the King Edward Hotel during the Beatles' visit. "That was crucial," Edith recalls. "Those kids outside in the street were just fooling themselves. What type of meaningful contact could

Signs of the times in Toronto.

they possibly have with the Beatles? From what we could hear in the lobby, it sounded like they were trying to kill them."

But the fifteen-year-old sisters knew hotel security would be tighter than the skin on Ringo's bass drum. "Obviously, we needed a room key," says Edith. "If we could flash a room key at hotel staff, then nobody would stop us from coming and going as we pleased."

During a preliminary reconnoitre of the King Edward's lobby, they discovered a drop box for keys that people forgot to leave at the front desk. "It was right by the lobby door. We put a fresh piece of bubblegum on the end of a thin stick and then, when no one was looking, fished out a key through the hole in the box."

Stage Two involved long hours of additional reconnaissance work spread over several more visits to the hotel. "We really cased the joint," Edith says. "We came to know every closet, every back door and stairs in the King Edward. We needed to know where to hide out if things got hot."

Finally, Stage Three. "The night of the Beatles' arrival, we dressed up in clothes that made us look older so we'd be less suspicious to the police and hotel guards. Then at about 11 o'clock we snuck out our bedroom window." Both of them were scared to death. If their hot-tempered Rumanian father had known what they were up to, he would have grounded them for months. "But Herta and I braced each other up," says Edith. "I've always believed that being twins gave us more courage than most young girls. It's easier to be brave when you have a partner in crime."

When they arrived downtown from their west end home, they showed their key to the guards and walked right into the lobby. "We were both stunned that everything was working out so perfectly. Then we sort of slinked to the back of the

LEFT:
George has a bumpy ride through the lobby of the King Edward Hotel.

77

***TOP MOVIES OF 1964 —
My Fair Lady; Mary Poppins;
The Unsinkable Molly Brown;
Hush, Hush, Sweet Charlotte;
A Hard Day's Night.***

A group of proud Canadians welcomes the Fab Four.

lobby and took up our positions by the elevator. Well, you knew the Beatles weren't going to take the stairs."

Although everything that happened next sped by in seconds, in Edith's memory it plays back only in slow-motion. After their entrance, the Beatles made for the elevators. Police locked arms to clear a path through the lobby. "All four were so close to us," says Edith. "First John went by, then Ringo, then George. By the time George came along I was so crazy that I burst through the line and grabbed his arm. 'George!' I screamed. Immediately several police grabbed me and knocked me to the ground. A boot heel – I'm sure it was George's – cut my hand. I picked the scab off that cut for months to keep it going, telling everyone that 'George did this to me.'"

While still down on all fours, Edith looked up to see Paul, her very favourite Beatle, coming towards her. "Somehow I managed to crawl through the legs of the police and stand up again right in front of him. Grabbing him by both hands, I cried, 'Paul, hi!' He smiled at me and said, 'Hello there, luv.'"

Edith stood frozen in a state of perfect bliss as she watched the elevator doors close behind Paul. Then what seemed like every girl in the lobby grabbed her and tried to kiss her hands. "You touched him! You touched him!" they shouted. Reporters moved in for an interview. "I told them, 'No way, I can't,'" Edith remembers. "'If my dad sees me, I'm dead.' Then the reporters laughed and said, 'Too late, everything you did is on film.' The next day we made the evening news and a couple of newspapers."

Once more, the twins found themselves in deep trouble. But Edith especially was too happy to care. Just two hours into the Beatles' Toronto visit, she not only proudly bore a wound courtesy of George's Cuban heel, but she had actually held Paul's hands and been addressed by him as "luv." Operation Beatles was a spectacular success.

"We were way beyond worrying about any punishment we might get," Edith says. "On the trip home, Herta and I agreed to be back at the hotel bright and early the next morning to try our luck again."

THE CHANT "WE WANT THE BEATLES" PENETRATED THE snug safety of the vice-regal suite from eight storeys below. The decibel level shot up every time even a curtain moved on the hotel's King Street front.

"Oh, they're getting a little excited down there," Paul said.

Snapped by the Beatle-Manea twins, Edith and Herta, this photo shows the street scene outside the King Edward Hotel on the day of the Toronto concerts.

· SEP · 64

"Stick your head out and give 'em a wave, mate," encouraged George.

"Not me, son," replied Paul. "I'm not for sticking my head out anywhere."

Although as many as thirty Toronto police and hotel detectives stood on guard on the eighth floor alone, security had nonetheless been breached in the Beatles' suite. A member of the entourage opened a linen closet to find a fourteen-year-old girl clutching a pillow and a blanket. She left quietly, without giving her name or saying how long she had been there.

The lads ordered up a snack of cheese sandwiches, crisp bacon and pots of tea, and settled in with a group of about twenty people, most closely connected with the show.

Several months before, the then-unmarried Elizabeth Taylor and Richard Burton, who had scandalized the world with the start of their affair on the set of *Cleopatra*, occupied the same rooms for seven weeks while Burton starred locally in a Broadway-bound production of *Hamlet*.

"I think it was lovely putting us in her suite," said John Lennon, no doubt tongue-in-cheek. "Thoughtful."

The three-bedroom vice-regal suite, which let for $85 a night, had recently been redone as part of a $2,500,000 renovation to the sixty-one-year-old hotel. Visitors entered a large drawing room furnished with exquisite Louis XV pieces, turquoise carpeting and a large chandelier. A mirror covered an entire wall; patterns of oriental silver adorned the other three. The hallway

LEFT:
A St. John Ambulance attendant carries off a fallen fan at the King Edward Hotel.

81

BELOW:
During their two-night stay at the King Edward, the Beatles occupied the same luxury suite that Elizabeth Taylor and Richard Burton had stayed in six months before.

82

leading to the bedrooms had gold-covered walls and a black-and-white tiled floor. One bedroom was done in white, one in beige-tinted white and one in mauve-grey. Two of the bedrooms had twin beds, while the third, the master bedroom, was outfitted with two doubles.

Gifts of all kinds, which had been pouring in for days, littered the drawing room – everything from flowers and fruit to candy, cakes and liquor (in New York, someone had sent them a five-week-old puppy, which was promptly turned over to the SPCA). A foot-high stack of fan mail sat ignored on the coffee table. The letters asked the boys to dinner, proposed marriage, urged John to divorce his wife, swore undying devotion and quite often included promises of sexual favours.

A few blocks north at Maple Leaf Gardens, a large crate of mail addressed to the Beatles sat in the office of Stan Obodiac, the arena's publicity director. An informal poll revealed that Ringo received about three letters to every one that came in for any of his mates.

One of them was opened by Gardens staff. In part, it read:
Dear Ringo:

Hi, how's your love life … sorry, I mean how's your life, love.
Hi again (I had to do the dishes for mom).
You will never believe this but I'm crying, 'cause suddenly I am faced with the frightening wonderful realization that in 34 days I see and I hope meet you.
Mom threatened to take me to a "head shrinker" when I told her that I know I was gonna meet you and you were gonna marry me because I rubbed your back.
I am so happy! I passed into grade 10 with 65 per cent (81 per cent last year) and I thought I would fail.
Please forgive my handwriting but I'm a Beatle wreck.
There was a postscript:

Crates of fan mail awaited the Beatles at their Toronto hotel and at Maple Leaf Gardens. Some letters proposed marriage; almost all swore undying devotion. This compendium of love letters to the Fab Four was published in 1964.

Mom got mad when I sent you my great uncle's penknife for luck…but who cares.

By the time the Beatles reached Toronto, just past the midway point in the tour, all four were fighting off the effects of colds that had nagged them ever since they left London. To keep going, they buffeted themselves with their favourite drink, J&B Scotch and Coca-Cola, and copious quantities of amphetamines.

The Beatles had picked up the speed habit in Germany during their early days playing the Kaiserkeller, a club in Hamburg's notorious Reeperbahn, the red-light district. There they honed their musical skills while performing virtually around the clock, with barely a break between sets and time off to sleep. The Beatles considered the popping of these pills harmless enough; just something to help get them through a hectic touring schedule that saw them criss-cross North America at an average rate of six hundred miles per day. Besides, amphetamines were perfectly legal and available over the counter at any pharmacy.

Days before, in the privacy of their suite at New York's Delmonico Hotel, Bob Dylan had introduced them to a new diversion that would also take hold. During this historic first meeting of the pop icons, Dylan was astonished to discover that none of the Beatles had ever smoked marijuana.

"But what about your song?" he asked. "The one about getting high?"

It seemed that in listening to "I Want to Hold Your Hand," Dylan misinterpreted the line "I can't hide" for "I get high."

After they all shared a good laugh, Dylan produced a large joint from his private stash and soon he and his hosts were puffing contentedly on a banned substance the Beatles would credit with broadening their minds as well as the horizons of

FLASHBACK TO '64…
April 25 — Toronto wins its third consecutive Stanley Cup with a 4-0 victory over Detroit in the seventh game of the finals.

83

How to Talk Like Ringo

GIRLS WERE "BIRDS." Something great, wonderful or fabulous was "fab" or "gear." A male might refer even to a contemporary as "son," and a good friend was neither a pal or a buddy, but rather a "mate."

Learning to talk just like the Beatles was all the rage during the heyday of the band. Kids spent hours trying to perfect the thick Scouse patois of the Fab Four's hometown of Liverpool. The basic idea, although few ever fully mastered the technique, was to constrict the nasal passage, throw the voice far back in the throat, and then let the words tumble forth in an adenoidal rush.

No one is quite certain how the uniquely Liverpudlian sound evolved. "Scouse" is derived from "lobscouse," the name of a local stew, which earned the city's inhabitants the nickname "Scousers." The slurring of vowels and the tone of the speech may be the result of the city's heavy air pollution from soot, which has long caused an unusually high rate of bronchial problems.

Most Canadian youngsters wisely confined their Beatle-talk to the popular handful of expressions already mentioned. But for the truly dedicated, there are dozens of other words and phrases still to be mastered.

For instance, in the Beatles hometown a Coke is still a soda pop, but "cokes" are restaurants, so called because they originally opened as cocoa rooms in the nineteenth century during a local anti-liquor crusade.

To "have a right cob on," for Liverpudlians as well as many other working-class Britons, is to be in a terrible mood. A "bevvy" is a drink, usually liquor. A "toff" is a rich man. A bloke might wear on his feet a pair of "daisy roots," which are boots. A suit of clothing is a "whistle and flute" or, more often nowadays, a "whicker."

There is a broad streak of sarcasm in Liverpudlian slang, an element often seen in the Beatles' humour. A "battler," for instance, is the popular name for someone who is overly timid. A slow-witted woman is known as a "Lively Polly." A "lino-chap" is someone who is always broke, or "on the floor."

It all gets a little confusing, which is why most fans content themselves with fab, gear and bird. To these should be added one final essential of Beatle-speak: "Tarra," as in "go happily" or "so long for now" John, Paul, George and Ringo, wherever you are.

their music. More than any other single event, that afternoon meeting at the Delmonico heralded the coming of a new psychedelic age.

Secluded with the Beatles in their suite at the King Edward Hotel were, as reporters delicately phrased it, "six unidentified young women." An endless supply of beautiful and willing females was one of the most delightful perquisites of their fame. Virile young men in their sexual primes, the Beatles took full advantage of the opportunities available to them. John Lennon later used one colourful word to describe the nightly debaucheries of that first North American tour – "Satyricon."

Sometimes local concert promoters arranged for visits by groupies or call girls. More often, Neil Aspinall, a longtime Beatles aide, would personally screen – and sometimes personally audition – the girls ushered into the inner sanctum. Aspinall usually chose from among the most promising prospects gathered in the hotel lobby, always making certain to check identity cards for proof of age. Sometimes as many as fifteen girls waited for entry into the Beatles' suite. Aspinall had them pass the time by ironing the Fab Four's stage costumes.

Before the next dawn, the girls would be handed autographed photos (inevitably forged by Aspinall, who had become expert at copying the Beatles' signatures), told to keep their mouths shut, and then ushered unceremoniously out the hotel's service entrance.

ABOUT 1:30 A.M., AFTER A POLICE SOUND TRUCK ANNOUNCED that the Beatles had gone to bed, the noise outside the King Edward finally began to subside. Minutes later the streets were almost deserted.

But less than six hours after that, a new contingent started collecting and by mid-morning a crowd estimated at

FLASHBACK TO '64...
April 28 – Vasily Vasihevich Tarasof, IzvESTIA correspondent in Ottawa, is expelled from Canada for espionage.

86

anywhere from two to three thousand was exuberantly crooning "O-Beatles" ("O Beatles, our idols true and dear...") on King Street.

Back again were the Beatle-Manea twins, who split their time soaking up the atmosphere and excitement in the street and roaming the halls of the hotel, hoping against hope to bump into the Beatles.

Several groups of teenage girls had pooled their resources to book rooms at the King Edward months in advance. Three sixteen-year-olds from Buffalo found themselves just five doors away from the Beatles on the eighth floor. The whole trip, including bus fare and meals, cost them $250. But they figured it was worth every penny. "I saw them!" one of them screamed. "It was worth $1,000 to see them."

But most hotel guests had to content themselves with just sleeping under the same roof as the adored ones. After the debacle of the night before, security was tighter than ever. Police and hotel guards completely sealed off the Beatles' floor to all uninvited visitors.

Decked out in matching, multi-hued sweaters that had the Beatles' names emblazoned on one side and "Yeah, Yeah, Yeah" on the other, cousins Cynthia Good, thirteen, and Ricky Stupp, ten, walked the halls of the King Edward kissing every doorknob on the off-chance that one of the Beatles had touched it. Ricky's mother had booked a room for the three of them as a special present for the girls. Cynthia and Ricky, thanks to a family friend with pull at Maple Leaf Gardens, had second-row seats for the concert that evening.

"Oh, the crazy things we did," Cynthia says. "I remember a very serious conversation with my cousin about whose hands looked most like Ringo's. We finally decided that hers did. So we took off all our rings and put them on one of Ricky's hands.

Dressed in matching Beatles sweaters, thirteen-year-old Cynthia Good and her cousin roamed the halls of the King Edward Hotel kissing every door knob on the off-chance that one of the Beatles had touched it.

Then we went to the window and watched the crowd on King Street go nuts when she put out her hand and waved. The noise was unbelievable. We kept doing it over and over for the feeling of power it gave us."

Cynthia and Ricky became obsessed with the idea that their room was directly over the Beatles' suite. "Of course, it probably wasn't, but we just knew that it was," says Cynthia. "That night we pulled all our covers off our bed and slept on the floor — just so we could be closer to them. I can still see the look on my poor aunt's face. She thought we'd both gone completely insane."

AROUND 11 A.M., FOR THE FIRST OF THREE TIMES THAT DAY, THE mob in the street gathered its strength and burst through the first police line in an attempt to get at the Beatles. Caught in the charge were Edith and Herta Manea. "Who knows what sparked it?" Edith says. "But suddenly people were racing towards the hotel like maniacs. We had no choice but to run along with the rest of them. If we'd stopped, we would have been trampled underfoot."

All these years later, Edith still feels guilty about something that happened during the stampede. "As we were running I stepped on the stomach of a girl who had fallen. I actually felt my foot kind of squish into her. I tried to turn back and find out how she was, but I kept getting swept back by the crowd. Even now I think about that and shudder."

A second line of cops mounted on motorcycles and horses just managed to turn back this first charge. Not long afterward, the Beatles themselves caused a momentary flutter by appearing at a window to wave and make sign language at a group of young women in the National Trust Building next door to the hotel.

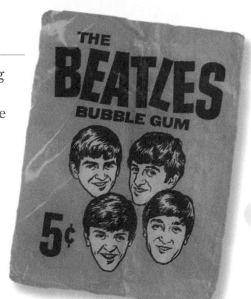

Five cards and a stick of stale bubble gum all for just five cents a pack…. These days Beatles cards sell for $1 to $2.50 apiece.

FLASHBACK TO '64…
May 17 — Prime Minister Pearson is roundly booed at a Royal Canadian Legion convention in Winnipeg when he discusses a new flag for Canada.

A teenager is hauled away to a first aid station as the crowd grows restless outside the King Edward Hotel.

"Normally we don't look out the windows because the fans go a little potty," explained Paul McCartney. "But we were amazed at seeing the girls there on Labour Day and gave them a cheery wave or two."

Nor was the euphoria of Beatlemania confined to the streets of downtown Toronto on the national holiday. Reports that the Fab Four might visit Niagara Falls before their Toronto concerts incited as many as four hundred teenagers in the border town to besiege the Seagram Tower, the local landmark that afforded a panoramic view of the Falls.

The crowd, which had begun gathering at dawn, dispersed early in the afternoon when it became clear the Beatles wouldn't show. But one sobbing girl vowed to return the next day – "just in case."

Outside the King Edward, several youngsters fainted in the suffocating humidity of 85-degree heat. These were handed over to a brigade of St. John Ambulance attendants, who had established a field camp in the King Edward's lobby. As the afternoon wore on, concerned parents arrived from the suburbs to retrieve their children. "These are my idiots," one mother said. "All right, that's enough."

In the relatively quieter moments, when they weren't girding for another run at the police lines, some of the youngest girls (the crowd's composition was overwhelmingly female) reached out to the constables as if to their fathers – politely asking for a cup of water, hugging their arms and tearily wiping their cheeks against the policemen's uniforms.

Everyone agreed Toronto cops performed magnificently throughout the visit. Vancouver and Montreal forces had only to cope with the hysteria for a scant few hours. But in Toronto, where Beatlemania put down deeper roots than anywhere else in Canada, police stood on guard through two long nights and two sold-out concerts.

Almost as if wishing it would make it so, police chief James Mackey had predicted that Toronto the Good was not likely to experience the level of mayhem seen in other cities on the tour. "The people of Toronto have more self-control than that," he insisted.

In fact, keeping the peace during the Beatles' stay would require almost every man and woman at the Toronto force's disposal. Brought in from all Metro divisions – and leaving each one shorthanded as a result – about

FLASHBACK TO '64...
May 24 — Eighty-five are arrested in Montreal during anti-Victoria Day demonstrations.

FAR RIGHT:
Dozens of Beatles fan magazines filled the newsstands in 1964. This assortment was gathered for a story that ran in the Toronto Telegram.

thirteen hundred police worked twelve- and sixteen-hour shifts. This small army of constables, who individually made an average of $2.50 an hour, worked ninety-six hundred hours of overtime during the Labour Day weekend.

"I like these guys," Inspector Harold Adamson, one of Mackey's top men and himself a future chief, would say of the Beatles before the weekend was through. "I think they're just fine, but will I be glad when they get the hell on that plane out of here. I haven't slept in three days."

The second of the day's three attempts by fans to crash through police lines and storm the doors of the King Edward occurred at 1:37 p.m. Like the first try that morning, this was an apparently spontaneous outburst. Men passing by on the sidewalk rushed to help police form a human chain and stem the tide.

Inside the vice-regal suite, the Beatles enjoyed a late lunch, scanned the newspapers from home (aides always made certain to have the London dailies on hand) and then slowly got ready to depart for Maple Leaf Gardens. The first concert began at 4 p.m., but they weren't due on stage until 5:30. The Beatles would conduct a press conference on the arena floor before the start of the second show at 8:30 p.m.

Summoned to their suite, the King Edward's resident physician, Dr. Edward Foreman, examined all four of the ailing Beatles, but gave John and George, who felt the worst, an especially thorough going-over.

Pronounced the doctor: "They've got bad colds but they're like race horses, raring to go."

It was time for the Beatles to leave the safety of their plush cocoon. At 4:15, when five black limousines pulled up at the hotel's front door, three thousand young girls braced for action. Police strained to hold them back while the cars stood empty for ten interminable minutes. And then, when several figures emerged from the hotel and got into all but the lead limo, all hell broke loose.

Kids swarmed over and under and around the cops, puncturing the line in a dozen places. They swept across the road and engulfed the limousines. Weeping in disappointment at what they discovered, they then angrily pushed a few feet further on and tried to beat down the King Edward's doors.

The men in the limousines were mere newsmen and Beatles aides. Their appearance, preceded by the arrival of the cars a few minutes before, was all part of an elaborate ruse hatched by police to deliver the Beatles out of the hotel and on to Maple Leaf Gardens.

At that very moment, John, Paul, George and Ringo, after descending from the eighth floor in a service elevator, were racing through a kitchen door and into a grey police paddy wagon parked at the rear of the hotel, just inside the garage door. The door rolled up and the paddy wagon gunned out of the hotel, first heading east and then turning north on the short hop to the Gardens.

Only about twenty youngsters who happened to be passing the garage door on their way to the front of the hotel realized

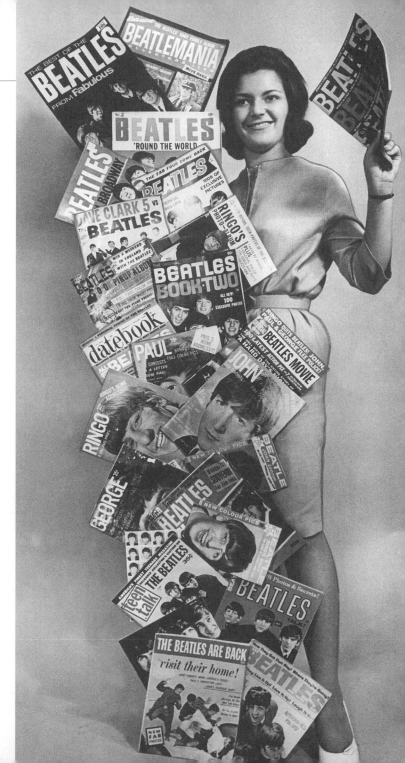

what was going on. Several gave chase for a hundred feet or so before being left behind.

George Harrison later protested that he and the other Beatles had been perfectly willing to come out of the King Edward's front door and run the gauntlet of their fans. Always an outspoken critic of what he considered overzealous police officials, Harrison said the fans who had waited for so long in the sweltering heat deserved the opportunity to see them. But police chief Mackey had insisted on the paddy wagon.

In their wake the Beatles left at least thirty-five girls swooning from a combination of exhaustion, heat stroke and hysteria; no serious injuries, but the King Edward's lobby looked, in the eyes of one reporter, "like a wartime emergency hospital with the prostrate bodies of girls lying on cots or just on the carpeted floor, while more than a dozen St. John Ambulance men and women comforted them."

MONTREAL POLICE WOULD LIKEWISE RESORT TO SUBTERFUGE THE next day in delivering the Beatles from the airport to the Forum.

Small groups of teenagers began gathering outside the hockey shrine at 10 a.m. When hooligans among them started scrawling slogans on walls and pounding on doors, cops ordered them to move on. By 1:45 p.m., the crowd on the sidewalks numbered about five hundred. Despite a heavy downpour, most stubbornly stayed put, determined to catch a glimpse of the Beatles when they arrived.

Though so thick on the ground that they literally formed a human wall around the Forum, police took no chances. Using a variation on the fake limo trick seen in Toronto, they dispatched a black airport taxi carrying four Beatle-bewigged police rookies to the Forum's front door at about 2:40 p.m.

The taxi drew the attention of every fan in the vicinity, including the one hundred or so standing near the Forum's back entrance. When they dashed to the front to see what was going on, police sealed off the area. Seconds later the three limousines carrying the Beatles and their entourage braked to a halt in front of the rear door. The lads stepped safely inside the Forum without muss or fuss before the kids out front fully realized they'd been had.

ONE OBSERVER REMEMBERED WATCHING A STUNNED NATHAN Cohen, the *Toronto Daily Star*'s dignified drama critic, who was more used to sedate opening nights at Stratford, bobbing like a cork in a sea of youngsters as he tried to make his way towards Maple Leaf Gardens for the first concert Monday afternoon.

Adrift on the same tide was ace *Globe and Mail* photographer Boris Spremo. "One kid in the crowd handed me a piece of tissue and asked me if I would touch the Beatles with it and hand it back to her," Spremo remembers. "What do you say to something like that? The kid looked like she would cry if I said no. So I took the tissue and told her I'd do my best."

Thousands waited to greet the Beatles in the streets outside the Gardens. The crowd began building early that morning. Some fans, too hyper to stand still and hoping to keep abreast of any late-breaking developments, spent the hours wandering the streets between the arena and the King Edward Hotel.

The Beatles were front-page news across Canada and around the world.

NIGHT EDITION

TORONTO DAILY STAR

METRO WEATHER
Mainly sunny and warm. High today, 85; low tonight, 65.

ESTABLISHED 1892

July paid circulation 339,488 copies per day   Tuesday, September 8, 1964 — 56 pages   10c per copy, 60c per week home delivery

200 girls swoon in battle of the Beatles

76 arreste as Montrea mob burns Union Jacl

By RAY TIMSON
Star Staff Writer

THEY'RE gone today —and all our children are accounted for. Our airport is still standing. So's the Gardens. And the King Eddy.

But if THEY ever return, there's only one hope: A vaccine against them.

THEY'RE the BEATLES, of course— four lively exports from Liverpool, England, who emit raucous .

● For other Beatle pictures and stories see pages 2, 3, 5, 18, 22 and 23.

sounds nowadays called songs, evoke polite applause in the form of faints and fits, and otherwise occupy themselves by playing Rockefeller roulette — a money - counting game in which every bill under $100 is thrown away.

FRENZIED TEENAGE GIRLS strained with might and main but were foiled in their attempt to break through police lines at the King Edward hotel when their idols, the Beatles arrived in Toronto for two shows. The quartet had to take a police paddy wagon from hotel to Maple Leaf Gardens to avoid howling crowd.

MONTREAL (CP)—Youths carrying flags ing revolutionary slogans staged a rowdy der last night in midtown Montreal — burning U and overturning three cars.

Police arrested 76 and said they will be c disturbing the peace, refusing to obey poli disperse and holding a parade without a pe point the mob was estimated at 300.

The disturbance erupted when the demonstrators marched to Lafontaine Park, where 46 Separatist sympathizers clashed with police last week.

Police were tipped off in advance and used mounted policemen to break up the parade.

But an hour later the youths, carrying Quebec fleur de lis and French Tricolor flags, reassembled.

FLAG BURNED
A Union Jack was burned at the foot of the Dollard des Ormeaux monument and several more set afire of a building oc-

Beatles' blonde snubs mayor
Mayor Philip Givens couldn't get to see the Beatles.

The mayor and his wife called at the singers' hotel suite at 1.30 a.m. today to pay their respects. According to the mayor, they got "a very rude reception." when he knocked, the

Holi ends deat for

OTTA
Accide
Labor
least
The
the b

The lads laze as the girls scream

FAR RIGHT:
An ad from a Montreal newspaper for the Beatles' afternoon concert at the Forum, along with a local radio station's rundown of that week's chart toppers.

BELOW:
The scene outside Maple Leaf Gardens before the afternoon show.

Rumours regularly popped up that the Beatles would arrive at any moment. Each time, a current of excitement charged the street. The screaming intensified; tired arms raised their home-made signs and store-bought pennants higher in the air. Fans reacted to almost anything. When a group of policemen left their posts for a lunch break, some youths, taking it as a sign that the Beatles were coming, started fighting their way forward for a better look.

For reasons known only to himself, a truck driver carrying a sign reading "I Hate The Beatles" waded bravely into the crowd. A mighty cheer arose when a girl snuck up from behind and snatched the placard out of his hands.

At 2:30 p.m., the Gardens opened its doors to ticket-holders for the opening concert. This considerably thinned the ranks of the Beatles' reception committee. But soon the crowd began to build again with the early arrival of eager ticket-holders to the second show.

Unaware of recent events at the King Edward, everyone outside the Gardens still expected the Beatles to arrive in their black limousines. So only a few dozen fans and a handful of photographers took notice when around 4:30 a paddy wagon cruised slowly to a back entrance of the arena. Before they knew what had happened, the gate swung open, the paddy wagon turned in and the gate slammed shut again.

Proof once more that the only sure way to see the Beatles was to buy a ticket.

CKGM Picks The Hit

1. Hard Days Night .... Beatle
2. Everybody Loves Somebody .... Dean Martin
3. Wishin' and Hopin' .... Dusty Springfield
4. Such A Night .... Elvis Presley
5. Rag Doll .... Four Seasons
6. Handy Man .... Del Shannon
7. Dang Me .... Roger Miller
8. Where Did Our Love Go .... Supreme
9. Walk Don't Run .... Ventures
10. How Glad I am .... Nancy Wilson
11. Little Old Lady .... Jan and Dean
12. Girl From Ipanema .... Getz and Gilberto
13. People Say .... Dixie Cups
14. How Do You Do It .... Gerry and Pacemakers
15. Angelito .... Rene and Rene

THE BEATLES
APPEARING AT THE
MONTREAL FORUM
TUESDAY, SEPT. 8th
AFTERNOON TICKETS STILL AVAILABLE FOR 4 P.M. PERFORMANCE
ADMISSION $4.50 and $5.50
TICKETS NOW ON SALE AT THE FORUM BOX OFFICE MONDAY TO FRIDAY FROM 10 A.M. TO 5 P.M.
MAIL ORDERS WILL BE ACCEPTED
SORRY! Evening Performance
Sold Out

Wowing the Press Chapter 4

"**I WONDER IF I SHOULD** give up newspaper work," pondered reporter Peter Desbarats after *The Montreal Star* assigned him to the Beatles beat.

"You have my sympathy, Mac," his taxi driver offered when he got out at the Forum.

Columnist Bruce West of *The Globe and Mail* insisted that he only attended the Beatles' press conference at Maple Leaf Gardens because he had been ordered there by his teenage daughter, who demanded a full report.

"I naturally wouldn't think of going to a Beatles press conference for the world," West wrote. "One of my troubles was that, except for Ringo, I could never really be sure which Beatle was which. I know Ringo, because he's the homely one."

Like Desbarats and West, most journalists, too old or too

PRECEDING PAGES:
The Beatles hold court at the Toronto press conference.

unhip to appreciate the musical and cultural significance of four shaggy-haired invaders from Britain, complained loudly about their assignments. They insisted, often in print, that all rock music was unmelodious trash. Those who never learned to tell one Beatle from another wore their ignorance like a badge of honour.

Most who attended the concerts and press conferences in Vancouver, Toronto and Montreal came determined to dislike the Beatles on sight. But prodded by their editors and sometimes even by teenage daughters, they did come – and in record numbers. For the truth was that by now Beatlemania had reached the point where the press needed the Beatles far more than the Beatles needed the press. These, after all, were the four lads who had taken the world by storm. A close-up look might reveal how they'd managed it.

Writers, photographers, disc jockeys, cameramen and television personalities, including many of the best-known media figures in the country, braved the hordes to meekly present their credentials at the door.

In Vancouver, where the site of the press conference was shifted at the last minute from the Hotel Georgia to Empire Stadium, eighty-nine of them squeezed into a suffocatingly humid little room designed to hold less than half that many. Included were travelling Beatles correspondents from the London *Daily Mirror* and the *Liverpool Echo*, as well as reporters from several major U.S. papers.

Paul McCartney turns on the charm in Vancouver.

103

Far larger audiences attended the press conferences held between the shows in Toronto and Montreal, where the Beatles held forth from behind four microphones set on tables placed on the stage. In Toronto alone, more than a thousand applications arrived for special press courtesies. Dozens of American girls wrote to W. Park Armstrong, United States Consul in Toronto, asking him to intervene on their behalf. One requested help from an even higher authority, President Lyndon Johnson.

"Everyone claimed to be relatives of someone in the Beatles' camp," remembers Paul White, the Capitol Records executive who had championed the Beatles in Canada. "People even learned the names of the roadies and claimed to be connected to them. Little girls would send in notes written in pencil saying, 'Please, can you send me a press pass.' My phone was ringing off the hook."

Bruce West wrote of the scene at Maple Leaf Gardens: "There were assembled more reporters, cameramen and radio announcers than I'd ever seen at a press conference before – and that's counting some for President F. D. Roosevelt and Prime Minister W. S. Churchill."

Significant numbers of policemen, firemen and St. John Ambulance attendants further swelled the ranks around the stages in Toronto and Montreal. And at some point every janitor, usher and concessionaire in the buildings abandoned their posts to sneak a peek at the proceedings.

From their elevated position on stage, the Beatles looked down over the assembled newsmen. They appeared jolly and relaxed, "with a fine ironic sense that this arrangement was fit and proper," noted one reporter. "Like four ancient kings," added another. "With the subjects down below squirming for a better look – groping for words to get into the conversation – pushing to get a microphone within earshot…"

Press-conference attendees at Empire Stadium stewed in their own juices for forty minutes before the Beatles finally made their entrance. At any other time, hard-nosed newshawks in the crowd would have stomped out in disgust – but not today.

The Beatles nonchalantly explained that they had needed the time to finish the cheeseburgers and chicken wings purchased on the drive from the airport, and to drink their tea.

From city to city, the routine never varied. Before the Beatles' arrival, Derek Taylor, the group's press officer, would start by reading two or three humorous telegrams from fans. A handsome young rogue of prodigious charm, Taylor had been a theatre critic in Manchester when one night he kicked down the band's dressing-room door to introduce himself and ask a question. The display of bravado and his quick wit instantly won over the Beatles and Brian Epstein, who hired him as his assistant and publicist.

A man in Saskatchewan had sent a wire requesting a few quarts of the Beatles' bath water, Taylor told his appreciative Toronto audience. No explanation as to why.

From a female Beatlemaniac came a cable inquiring about George's recent

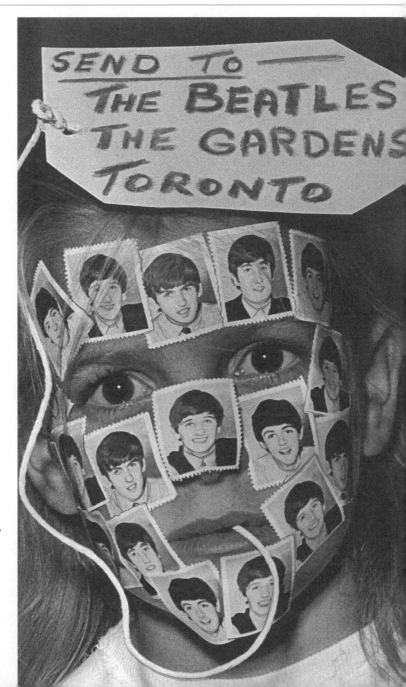

throat trouble. Would it be possible to have his tonsils should they need to be removed?

Without further ado, Taylor brought the Beatles, who waved and smiled amiably, onto the stage to general applause. In Toronto and Montreal, they wore fresh clothes after changing out of their stage costumes following the opening concerts. The Beatles spent the next few minutes striking poses for the photographers – standing, sitting behind their microphones, individually, as a group.

Photographer Boris Spremo takes the measure of Paul, Ringo, George and John during the Toronto press conference.

"The press conference was extremely well run," remembers Toronto photographer Boris Spremo. "Nobody rushed us and there was plenty of room on the stage for everyone. But what really impressed me was the professionalism of the Beatles. Nowadays you get these prima donna rock stars who say, 'Okay, we'll give you one minute to get your shots.' But the Beatles weren't like that at all. They were very patient and really tried to give us what we needed."

Though accommodating, the Beatles weren't about to let themselves be pushed around. In Toronto, they comically swatted away a camera crew from the new CBC magazine show "This Hour Has Seven Days," when a grip kept slamming a clap-board in their faces to record the various scenes and takes.

By now the press-conference drill was second nature to the Fab Four. The instant Derek Taylor announced the end of the general photo session, they erased their grins and turned their backs to the cameras.

Next came what Taylor liked to call the "presentations." This was when disc jockeys, beauty queens, record-company

1966
PRESS CONFERENCE PASS
for the BEATLES
6:30 pm – Aug. 17

* * * CONDITIONS FOR ADMISSION

— Pass good for press conference ONLY.

— NO ONE UNDER 18 YEARS WILL BE ADMITTED.

— Only full-time reporters to be admitted.

— No autographs to be requested.

— No one allowed backstage.

— Photographers should fly their lapel photo pass besides this general pass.

(IMPORTANT — Gather in the EAST lobby for instructions as to location of press conference.)

(Admission by this card ONLY. ONE admission per card. Carry in hand or, preferably, tie to button-hole.)

N? 287

Spremo's pass for the 1966 press conference at Maple Leaf Gardens.

executives and sundry other local notables got their chance to pose with the boys and sometimes make a brief statement.

One of those brought forward into the spotlight at the Toronto press conference was fan club president Trudy Medcalf. "Even after all these years, I can still remember my little speech," she says. "'On behalf of the largest Beatles fan club in Canada, I want to welcome you to the city. We love you all very much.' At that point Paul McCartney put his hand on my shoulder and joked, 'Oh, you don't, do you?' I was thrilled and completely flustered, but somehow I managed to go on with my speech. 'We hope you remember your visit to Toronto very fondly.'"

This was Trudy's second meeting with the Beatles, and both times Paul played the tease. In February when the Beatles landed in New York to appear on "The Ed Sullivan Show," radio station CHUM, the fan club's sponsor, sent Trudy to meet her idols. She was helping to sort fan mail in their suite at the Plaza Hotel when the boys trooped in. "When John Lennon found out that I was with the fan club, he got down on his knees and bowed to thank me. The Beatles seemed so excited and amazed at their reception in New York. They all had such youthful enthusiasm. Ringo, I remember, was flinging elastic bands around the room."

Paul did a double take when he saw what Trudy was wearing. "I had on a pair of culottes, you know, pants cut to look

A page from a British fan club magazine shows Ontario fan club president Trudy Medcalf and another girl helping to sort mail in the Beatles' suite before the band's first appearance on "The Ed Sullivan Show."

like a skirt," Trudy says. "Paul started playing with the fabric and said, 'Are these pants, luv? I really like them.' I almost died on the spot. Can you imagine the thrill for a young girl of having Paul McCartney do something like that?"

At Empire Stadium, a group of West Vancouver high-school girls presented the Beatles with a four-foot-tall Ookpik, a round-headed, pointy-nosed stuffed toy of vaguely Inuit

The Toronto press conference was Trudy's second meeting with the Beatles, and both times Paul played the flirt.

origins that had inexplicably become a national rage. The mayor of Kingston, Ontario, journeyed to Toronto to proclaim the lads honorary citizens of his city. But the highlight of the Toronto press conference, at least as far as the Beatles were concerned, had to be their meeting with the reigning Miss Canada, a gorgeous blonde from Newfoundland with whom they would rendezvous later that night in their suite at the King Edward.

Occasionally at these gatherings – or sometimes backstage just before the start of a concert – disabled young people were brought forward to receive a blessing of sorts or a healing touch from the hand of a Beatle. All four were appalled by such acts of irrational reverence, but especially John. As an angry young art student back in Liverpool, he had taken special delight in tormenting the disabled. "Where's ya legs go, mate?" he'd call to an amputee on the street. "Run away with your wife?"

North American tour promoters often placed disabled youngsters directly in front of the stage. Flashbulbs and the glare of stage lighting prevented the Beatles from seeing more than a few rows into their audiences. All agreed that their most disturbing memory of the tour was looking out night after night at what appeared to be arenas filled only with people in wheelchairs.

The time finally came for the Beatles to take questions from the audience. Supremely confident behind their micro-

111

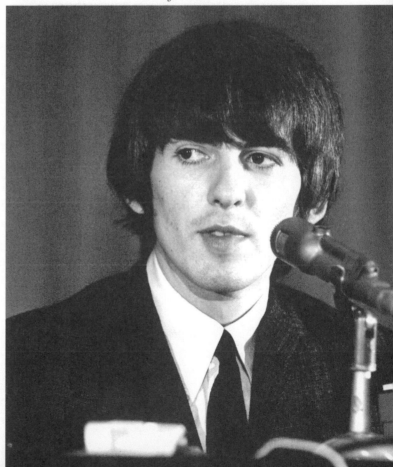

RIGHT:
The lads seem distracted despite the presence of Miss Canada, Mary Lou Farrell.

phones, they did their best to answer every question with a combination of good humour and saucy Liverpudlian charm. A glib or funny reply had long since been honed for every imaginable query.

Paul McCartney told the Vancouver assembly that the group would be starting another movie in February. George Harrison piped in that they had no title for it yet. Ringo Starr added that they had no story for it yet. John Lennon said they had no actors for it yet.

"How much money do you make collectively?" asked a Toronto reporter.

"A lot," answered John.

"Will you leave show business when you have made enough to leave?"

"We've made enough to leave now, but we're not going to," John replied.

"We're greedy," added George.

"What time do you get up in the morning?"

"Two o'clock in the afternoon," said John.

"It's been said that you appeal to the maternal instinct in these girls."

"It's a dirty lie."

Naturally, reporters tried their best to cover all the local and national angles.

But the Beatles confessed that they hadn't the foggiest notion of what an Ookpik might be.

Canadian girls? "They're fine," shrugged Paul. "Like girls anywhere, I guess."

A questioner in Montreal wondered if they would like to appear in other Canadian cities. The answer came that they would "appear anywhere if the people have enough money."

Also in Montreal, a French-speaking reporter asked, "Do

The Boom in Beatles Memorabilia

THAT FOURTEEN-INCH Beatle comb you bought at Eaton's Beatle Bar back in 1964 for 49 cents nowadays sells for upwards of $100. The Fab Four lunch box you proudly toted to school fetches $350 to $400 (add another $100 or so for the matching thermos). And the set of nodding Beatle dolls that your mother dismissed as dust collectors and finally tossed in the garbage might now have been worth as much as $1,000.

"All this stuff is just exploding in value," says Peter Miniaci, the owner of The Beatlemania Shoppe in Toronto. "Baby boomers come into my store with Beatle items they've discovered in their basement or attic and are just amazed by what they're worth."

Miniaci figures prices will go even higher. "Why not? The success of the *Anthology* releases has the band right back on top. The Beatles' movie *Let It Be* and the *Yellow Submarine* cartoon are both being re-released on video. That will generate even more excitement."

So start scouring your storage spaces for forgotten Beatle treasures. A mint-condition, first-edition copy of John Lennon's *In His Own Write*, his thin volume of

verse and doodles, is worth about $100. Old Beatles magazines in good shape can bring $15 to $25 per copy. Beatles cards, which used to cost 5 cents a pack, now go for $1 to $2.50 each.

If your search fails to turn up anything, then keep a watchful eye at flea markets and neighbourhood garage sales, both excellent sources. But be warned: Fab Four forgeries abound on the open market. It's important that the items have their original packaging to prove that they are genuine and not copies. "Original packaging adds as much as fifty per cent to the value," Miniaci says. Two names stamped on the product's label virtually guarantee authenticity: NEMS Enterprises Ltd. and Seltaeb (Beatles spelled backwards), which were the principal manufacturers of Beatles paraphernalia.

There's just one problem for serious buyers like Peter Miniaci. "People will come into the store with something really great, and just when I think I've made a deal, they change their minds," he says. "Their Beatle memories mean so much to them that they can't let go. I get a lot of that."

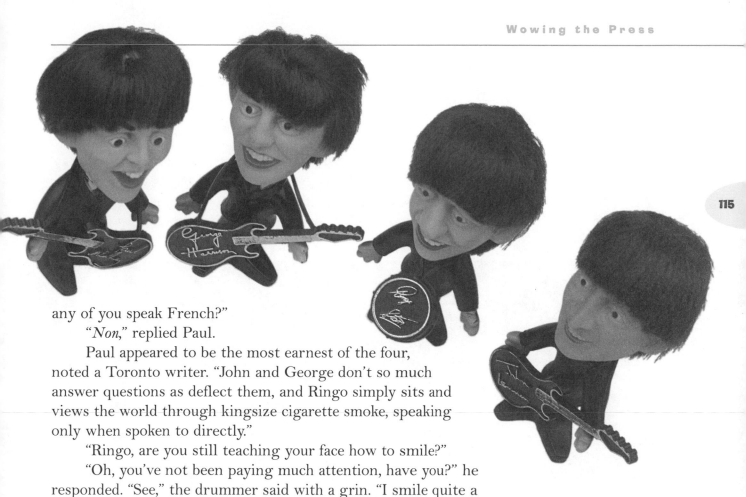

any of you speak French?"

"*Non,*" replied Paul.

Paul appeared to be the most earnest of the four, noted a Toronto writer. "John and George don't so much answer questions as deflect them, and Ringo simply sits and views the world through kingsize cigarette smoke, speaking only when spoken to directly."

"Ringo, are you still teaching your face how to smile?"

"Oh, you've not been paying much attention, have you?" he responded. "See," the drummer said with a grin. "I smile quite a lot."

Most of the questions were lobs the Beatles slammed out of the park. Only rarely was their patience tested or their tempers provoked. Even then, their wits never failed them.

Curmudgeonly Jim Fleming of Toronto radio station CFRB stood up and asked Ringo if he felt that any of the Beatles could talk for more than a minute on any given subject.

"There's one trying to be funny," said Ringo, pointing Fleming out to Paul.

FLASHBACK TO '64...
June 11 — Nelson Mandela receives a life sentence for sabotage and conspiracy to overthrow the government of South Africa.

"What's he, a wise guy?" muttered John.

Then someone asked, "How long do you think you'll last?"

"Longer than you, anyway," John sneered. There were no more sarcastic questions after that.

TRY AS THEY MIGHT TO RESIST, MOST REPORTERS CAME AWAY AS captivated as schoolgirls by the Beatles' quickness and cheek.

"It was really something to see," Red Robinson recalls of the reaction of the Vancouver press. "Within minutes the Beatles had all these tough guys laughing and eating out of

116

CBC-TV starlet Michele Finney interviews the Fab Four between concerts in Toronto.

their hands. Most of them had gone there hating their music and determined to slough off the Beatles as another passing craze. But it was impossible to just dismiss them. They had incredible charisma. Right away it was obvious to anyone who wasn't blind that here was something special."

"They had a relaxed, easygoing wit about them," happily conceded *The Globe and Mail*'s Bruce West. "Actually, they struck me as being pretty good kids, once you had a proper chance to peer at them underneath the shrubbery."

"You couldn't help but like them," agrees Boris Spremo. "They were four really humorous young guys. I think everyone there was charmed by them."

Despite all the money and fame and adulation heaped upon them at so young an age, none of it seemed to have gone to the Beatles' heads – at least not too noticeably. It was this natural modesty that most struck fourteen-year-old Michele Finney, the star of CBC-TV's "Razzle Dazzle" show. Finney was recruited by the *Toronto Daily Star* to observe and interview the Beatles between shows and report back with the Youthful Viewpoint.

Though she received three to four hundred fan letters of her own every week, Finney was as enamoured of the Beatles as any ordinary girl her age. She plastered her bedroom with photos of all four, although Paul was her favourite. She owned four of their five LPs, diligently kept a scrapbook on their exploits, belonged to their fan club and had once bought an entire carton of Beatle cards just to be certain of completing the set.

"I was used to dealing with big egos," Michele says today. "Being in show business you expect that – and I guess I thought the Beatles would be at least a little puffed up by their success. But I was really delighted by their naturalness. They weren't jaded at all, and still seemed in awe of their popularity."

Michele marvelled at her idols' patience during the press

TOP MOVIE BOX-OFFICE STARS OF 1964 — *Doris Day, Jack Lemmon, Rock Hudson, John Wayne, Cary Grant, Elvis Presley, Shirley MacLaine, Ann-Margret, Paul Newman, Jerry Lewis.*

RIGHT:
The Beatles spent the first minutes of the press conferences striking poses for the photographers.

conference, noting with maternal concern that Ringo appeared to be the first to tire. "Even though they smiled and appeared gay they still showed evident signs of stress," she wrote. "John, Paul, George and Ringo all looked like they needed a good helping of sun and relaxation."

During the intermission between the Toronto concerts, aides ushered Finney into the Beatles' backstage dressing room, where they were all intently watching a battle scene on TV. All four were smoking. Ringo had his feet up on the furniture and at one point "let out a huge, moaning bellow, for no apparent reason at all. John was chewing on cough pills."

Michele asked what they felt was their strongest audience appeal — their music or themselves?

"It's definitely the music," John answered.

Had they any explanation as to why millions of teenagers the world over had gone so completely ga-ga over them?

"People are always looking for idols," explained George. "In this age, it just happens to be us."

Finney felt pleased and relieved at having maintained her professional aplomb throughout the interview. "One reason the *Star* hired me was because I was a pro who could, they hoped, meet the Beatles without blubbering or fainting. And I did manage that while I was with them. I tried to think of it as just another performance."

But then the magnitude of what she'd experienced set in. "All my senses just sort of shut down," she says. "I was in a daze for at least two days, back to being a kid again — on the phone with all my girlfriends, talking for hours about what Paul was wearing or the way he laughed or smiled. All these years later, I still think of my meeting with the Beatles as one of the biggest thrills of my life."

IN TORONTO A REPORTER ASKED, "WHAT DO YOU THINK OF PRESS conferences?"

"They're great fun, aren't they?" John said.

"Has this tour been wearing you down?"

"It's been wearing us up," quipped George.

"It's nearly killed our road manager," added John.

"What do you miss most about England?"

From their elevated position on stage, the Beatles looked down over the assembled newsmen. "Like four ancient kings," observed one reporter.

120

"Hot tea," said George.

So many things about the Beatles were so radically different from anything that had appeared on the entertainment scene before – their Merseybeat sound, their hirsute appearance and their utter refusal to play the suck-up games that celebrities usually played with the press. This last innovation couldn't help

but endear them to the world-weary scribes assigned to their beat, each one convinced that he had seen and heard it all before.

"Do you worry about all these children collapsing at your shows?" the Beatles were asked in Toronto.

Another fat lob. This was where the Beatles were supposed to confess to spending sleepless nights fretting about the safety of their fans, and in dreaming up ways to solve the problem.

"No," John Lennon answered flatly. "We don't worry. They collapse but they get up again and walk away. No one's being seriously hurt. What's to worry?"

How about their own safety, then? "Do you ever worry when those wild crowds try to get at you?"

The politically correct answer to this one was that the Beatles selflessly put aside any concerns for their personal safety for the sheer joy of appearing before their beloved fans. It also wouldn't hurt to mention that, at any

FLASHBACK TO '64...
July 31 – The Ranger 7 spacecraft transmits the first close-up pictures of the moon's surface.

RIGHT:
While the Beatles met the press inside, outside Maple Leaf Gardens an anxious crowd gathered for the second show.

rate, they had complete faith in the local promoters and police to safeguard their protection.

But the Beatles were having none of it. "No," said George, no worries at all. Discussion closed.

A VANCOUVER QUESTIONER WONDERED WHAT THE BEATLES thought of Republican presidential candidate Barry Goldwater.

"He's not much fun, is he?" John threw back.

"What about the Queen?"

"She's all right," said John in Toronto. "Doin' a good job."

"When will you be knighted?"

"Next week," answered George.

ONE CANADIAN REVIEW OF *A HARD DAY'S NIGHT* RAVED THAT if the Beatles ever decided to abandon their music, they might instead become the next Marx Brothers. It was easy to share this vision as they held court at the press conferences. Their comedic timing and caustic edge were worthy of the great Groucho himself.

When a Vancouver radio reporter wondered how the boys felt "now that Britannia rules the airwaves," Paul McCartney jeered: "Oo, you worked that one out, didn't you!"

The Beatles absolutely refused to take themselves seriously. Nor, they insisted, should their fans put them on a pedestal and mimic their lifestyle.

"Do you worry about smoking in public?" someone asked in Toronto. "Do you think it might set a bad example for your younger fans?"

"We don't set examples," George answered. "We smoke because we've always smoked. Kids don't smoke because we do. They smoke because they want to. If we changed, we'd be putting on an act."

RIGHT:

The boys crack themselves up in Vancouver.

There was a pregnant pause as Ringo leaned towards his microphone and smiled.

"We even drink."

At all three Canadian press conferences, the Beatles worked the room like seasoned pros, intent on leaving their audiences laughing. A Vancouver reporter asked, "What's the most unusual request you've had?"

This one was taken by John, who smirked and answered, "I really wouldn't like to say."

Someone else in the same room asked Paul McCartney if he ever dated his fans. Certainly, said Paul, but he didn't think he could manage it during the Beatles' short stay in Vancouver.

"It would have to be a quick one," he added with a wink.

Concert of a Lifetime

Chapter 5

FIRST CAME A GUT-CHURNING, almost overwhelming build-up of anticipation, then sudden uncontrollable sobbing and hysteria, and finally the sense-numbing wall of noise likened by one writer to "a hundred jet engines being revved up at centre ice." Every moment, every sensation, is forever etched in the memories of those who were there.

"Never in all the years since have I been as emotionally high as I was during that concert," says Eric Twiname, the Montrealer who had guiltily switched allegiance from Buddy Holly to the Beatles. "The music and the charisma of the Beatles simply can't be matched. You couldn't take your eyes off them. I still compare every concert to that one. None have measured up."

"It's difficult to even describe my feelings," says Edith

PRECEDING PAGES:
The Beatles sprint for their limousine at the conclusion of the Vancouver concert.

Manea, one half of Toronto's Beatle-Manea twins. "I was exactly where I had dreamed of being for months. The screaming was so loud I could hardly hear anything they said or played. What I did hear of the music didn't sound nearly as good as their records. But I didn't go there to hear the music. I went to see them. And, my god, there they were."

John Lennon ripped into "Twist and Shout" to start the show.

129

A mixed bag of lesser lights opened the concerts, which started at 8:14 p.m. in Vancouver, and at 4:00 and 8:30 p.m. in Toronto and Montreal (the Montreal matinee actually got under way ten minutes late while Beatles aides rushed back to the airport to pick up forgotten stage costumes). MCs shamelessly exhorted audiences to show generous support for the opening acts, always remembering that each one had been personally selected by the Beatles.

The Bill Black Combo, a rock ensemble composed of singer, sax, guitar, drums and tambourine, came out first to polite applause. Like all the openers, they played just five songs. Next were The Exciters, three girls and a male singer who performed blues and gospel tunes. The third act on the card, at least in Toronto and Montreal, was Clarence "Frogman" Henry, whose vocal range wandered from a piercing falsetto shriek to the deep bass that earned him his nickname. At Vancouver's Empire Stadium and other stops early in the tour, the Righteous Brothers, two popular purveyors of so-called blue-eyed soul, filled the Frogman's spot. They reportedly dropped out because they couldn't tolerate the nightly uproar.

At this point, a fifteen-minute intermission interrupted the proceedings in Vancouver and Toronto. Montreal police, once again choosing to play it safe, insisted on eliminating the break. This was when disturbances had most often developed in other cities.

The audiences at both Montreal shows would later be described as among the best-behaved on the tour. Naturally, there was the usual screaming and weeping, but nothing like the sustained hysteria seen in Vancouver and Toronto. Although the second show sold out, the afternoon concert at the Forum attracted only 9,500 fans, well below the 11,500 capacity. That the concert fell on the Jewish High Holidays and the first day of school certainly didn't help.

During the intermission, hawkers strolled the aisles with soft drinks, ice cream, programmes and a variety of other Beatles souvenirs. The electricity and tension multiplied with every passing second. The lights darkened and out came the Bill Black Combo to play one more number. Then a sultry blonde, Kentucky-born singer-songwriter Jackie DeShannon, slinked onto the stage in a form-fitting dress. DeShannon was rumoured to be having an affair with John Lennon.

"DeShannon…seemed to activate her vocal chords by stamping, jerking her hips and urging the audience to shout with her," noted a disapproving reporter. Many adult onlookers felt her act too overtly sexual for so young an audience. A Vancouver policewoman near the stage called DeShannon's handling of the microphone disgusting. But when her five songs were over, the crowd was on its feet and cheering wildly for the first time. All previous acts had merely been tolerated. DeShannon made the walls shake.

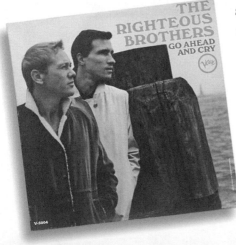

An early album of the Righteous Brothers, one of the opening acts for the Vancouver concert.

The preliminaries took precisely ninety minutes. The noise built to a heathen roar as stagehands dashed out to set up Ringo's drums or to test a guitar amplifier. Rows of police took up positions at the foot of the stage. The Toronto audiences even enthusiastically applauded when police inspector Jim Henderson, resplendent in his dress uniform, went onstage to warn that anyone not remaining seated would be ejected from the building.

The moment everyone had been imagining for months was

The crowd at Maple Leaf Gardens was ready to cheer anything, even police inspector Jim Henderson when he came on stage and warned them to stay in their seats.

131

so very close now. The MC bounded onto the stage to make the final introductions. Jungle Jay Nelson of Toronto's CHUM, who hosted the first Gardens show, unabashedly described this as the proudest moment of his life.

And then, with miraculous suddenness, John, Paul, George and Ringo appeared before them. The welcoming scream took anywhere from thirty-five seconds to a full minute to subside enough for the Beatles to start into their opening number, "Twist and Shout," with John shouting more than singing lead. A constant barrage of flashbulbs lit the darkness like firecrackers on Victoria Day. Girls shrieked and swayed. Almost all cried and many fainted dead away. The noise, wrote a Montreal reporter, "made a Stanley Cup crowd sound like nightingales. Veteran ushers at the Forum cowered and covered their ears."

In Vancouver, the moment the Beatles stepped out, at least a third of the more than eight thousand fans in the field-level seats rushed towards the stage. All that blocked their path was a suddenly flimsy-looking string of four-foot-high Beatle Baffles. Wedged between the fences and the stage were some eighty police, St. John Ambulance attendants, stadium guards and newsmen.

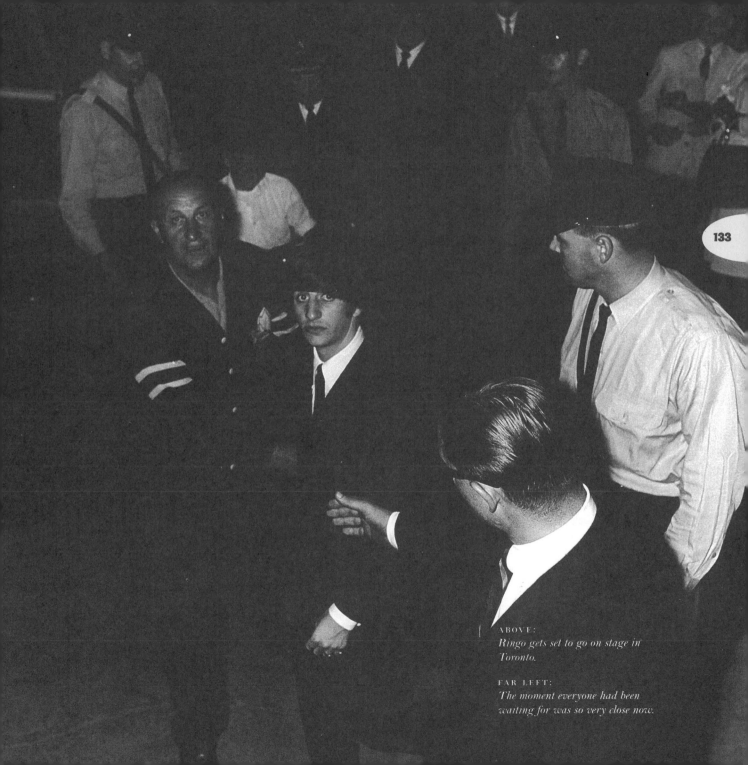

133

ABOVE:
Ringo gets set to go on stage in
Toronto.

FAR LEFT:
The moment everyone had been
waiting for was so very close now.

Police, who linked arms to brace the barrier when the first wave hit, just barely managed to hold on. Many of the fans who led the charge fell or were crushed against the fence. Police constantly waded in on search-and-rescue missions, pulling kids to safety and passing them into the waiting arms of the ambulance brigade.

"Ringo, Ringo! Don't take me away from Ringo," screamed

In Vancouver, thousands of fans rushed towards the stage the instant MC Red Robinson finished his introduction.

134

a thirteen-year-old girl, kicking furiously at the ambulance attendants as they carried her off for treatment at one of the stadium's two first-aid centres.

Della Darwin, a thirteen-year-old Vancouverite sitting eleven rows from the front, found herself lying flat on her back after having her bench seat upturned in the audience's rush to the stage. "My girlfriend and I had placed our bench on top of

Vancouver police called the scene at Empire Stadium the most unbelievable in the city's history.

135

another so that we could see better," she remembers. "Then, suddenly, whoosh, everything went out from underneath us.

"When I was lying there on the ground, all I could think about was climbing back to my feet so that I wouldn't miss another second of the concert. What was happening all around us didn't matter. My girlfriend hurt her head in the fall, but I even had trouble working up any concern over that. I was literally screaming my throat raw. I couldn't speak for two days afterward. I was so focused on the stage that everything else just blanked out."

Meanwhile, outside Empire Stadium, hundreds of ticketless youngsters massed for an assault on the twelve-foot-high northwest gate. The mob had been growing in size and courage for the last hour or so. Three times they flung themselves against the heavy wooden gate before it finally crashed down. About twelve teenagers scrambled through. Police and stadium workmen hurriedly reinforced the doorway with heavy supporting boards. Together they managed to prop it back up.

The stadium's south-end entrance was also under siege. There, several more teenage boys squeezed past before police sealed the gap. One cop was slightly injured. Later in the evening, another would be attacked and three fist fights

FAR LEFT:
Ecstasy!

BELOW:
Smiles all around backstage at Maple Leaf Gardens while out in front the MC makes the final introductions.

broke out. Two nineteen-year-olds and an adult were arrested and charged with intoxication.

The pitched battles outside Empire Stadium made no sense. Teenage hooligans – there not for any love of the Merseybeat but only to make trouble – had to be the instigators. For in truth, right until showtime thousands of tickets, priced from $3.25 to $5.25, remained unsold. Nobody with the price of admission needed to fight his way in.

Despite perfect weather, only 20,621 filed into a stadium capable of seating 27,000 for a show of this type. The Pacific National Exhibition, which had counted on a big pay-off, barely broke even on the event.

Many fans may have stayed away because of Empire Stadium's notoriously bad acoustics. Some in Vancouver thought that the PNE hadn't done all it could to sell the show. But this hardly seems fair. How much more promotion could the phenomenally popular Fab Four need?

Red Robinson, the concert's master of ceremonies, has his own theory. "It's all a question of demographics," he says. "In 1957, twenty-five thousand kids turned out to see Elvis Presley at Empire Stadium. But that group had aged and weren't interested in something new like the Beatles. In my opinion, there just weren't enough twelve-to-fifteen-year-old girls to go around, not in Vancouver anyway. The slightly older kids would catch on to the Beatles soon enough. But in 1964 most of their following consisted of very young girls."

What the Beatles' West Coast audience lacked in size, it made up in dangerously

139

LEFT:
Up the stairs and out into the glare of a thousand flashbulbs at Empire Stadium.

BELOW:
Edith Manea, the Beatle-Manea twin, snapped this shot of the Fab Four's stage set-up in Toronto.

unbridled enthusiasm. Vancouver police agreed the noise and general rowdiness exceeded even that of the Elvis concert, which had set the old standard. Some people called the Beatles' appearance the most unbelievable scene in the city's history.

"There's no comparison with any other crowd I've seen," Vancouver Police Inspector Bud Errington said in the noise and confusion of the night. "These people have lost all ability to think."

Errington put in a call for police dogs and handlers to help safeguard the

RIGHT:
Police strain to hold back the throng in Vancouver.

BELOW:
While battling his way to the front, teenager Jim Beckstead took this photo of the stage at Empire Stadium.

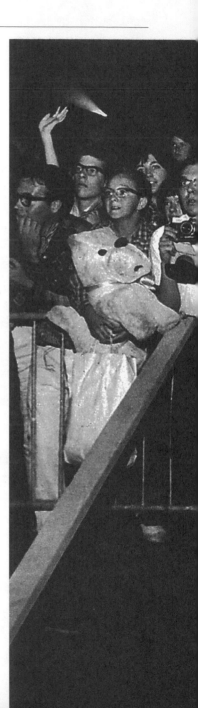

142

Broadcast live by local radio station CKNW, the Vancouver concert was illegally taped by a fan. The recording was later released in the form of this exceptionally rare two-record "bootleg" album.

south and northwest gates. He also urgently ordered additional men to bolster the line in front of the stage, which looked as if it might break at any second.

FOR THE BEATLES, THE SCREAMING AND THE SOBBING AND EVEN the rioting all made for just another day at the office.

"Even though they know they are not being heard they sing enthusiastically," noted the *Toronto Daily Star*'s Nathan Cohen. "They make mild jokes, funny even though they are usually inaudible. John Lennon mimics Paul McCartney's teasing request for the audience to clap hands loudly, otherwise they might not hear them. Paul whirls around and hoists his guitar high, knowing this will set the girls aflame. Ringo Starr bangs the drums and tosses his mane of hair, another signal for pandemonium. George Harrison executes his leggy gyrations with grace and reserve."

The noise, especially in Vancouver and Toronto, seldom waned. When it did, one of the Beatles would do something adorable and the uproar began again. The loudest cheers were reserved for Ringo, whose vocalizing on "Boys" was completely drowned out by the crowds.

With a lunatic's death threat hanging over his head, Ringo recalled the Montreal concerts as "the worst gig of my life." A police detective sat partially hidden behind the drum riser next to him. "God knows what he was going to do," Starr said. "I mean, there's an assassin out there trying to get me and he's sitting next to me on stage as if someone in the back of a 12,000-seater is gonna go – *Bang!* – and he's gonna catch the bullet?"

While thousands at the Forum cried out his name, Ringo crouched low behind his drum set, trying to make himself as inconspicuous as possible, hoping that his cymbals might deflect any lead fired his way. "No one," he said, "was seeing much of me that day."

Most who were at the concerts say they could hear almost nothing above the screams. The puny, primitive amplifiers of the day barely projected the band's music beyond the front

143

MC Red Robinson brings the Beatles on stage in Vancouver.

rows. What could be heard of the vocals often sounded off-key. Many nights on the tour the musicianship was nothing short of dreadful.

Even this early in their fame, the Beatles were growing frustrated with trying to make themselves heard by audiences who loved them too much to bother listening. In the past, John had sometimes tried to quiet the crowds by shouting at them to "Shaaaaarup!" Now he was more likely to move just off the mike and scream obscenities. Ringo recalled that sometimes all four of them would suddenly stop playing in the middle of a song.

144

Most who were at the concerts said they could hear almost nothing above the screaming.

Nobody ever noticed.

"I know I was a little disillusioned by their performance," says Martin Black, then a fifteen-year-old in the audience at Toronto's evening concert. "Everything was off-key – their voices, their instrumentals. Not that you could really blame them. The screaming was unbelievable and acoustics at the Gardens were terrible to begin with. Don't get me wrong. I still felt that it was a terrific show; an experience I'll never forget. But I remember thinking that the Bill Black Combo, one of the lead-in acts, sounded a whole lot better and more professional than the Beatles."

Maybe it just wasn't the Fab Four's night. Montrealer Eric Twiname, who like Martin Black went on to become a professional musician, recalls how good the Beatles sounded the next day during their first show at the Forum, where the audience was at least a little quieter. "I was way up in the rafters, but they sounded crisp and dead on to me," he says. "I thought they gave a great concert."

THE SOLID WALL OF SCREECHING YOUNGSTERS – ONE HUNDRED feet deep and stretched across the width of the field – continued to test the strength and endurance of the police manning the stage-front barricades at Empire Stadium. Inspector Errington had two hundred of his huskiest men in place by now, but still the line threatened to collapse.

One constable pulled newsmen aside to show them a spot under the stage where they'd be safe if the fans broke through. At the same time a sergeant hastily made plans to evacuate the Beatles from the stadium in the rear of a truck.

Paul McCartney greets Toronto with his camera at International Airport.

Jungle Jay introduces the BEATLES to Toronto.

The two photos on this back cover from a CHUM Chart of the time show the band arriving at the Toronto airport and their introduction by MC Jungle Jay Nelson at the afternoon concert.

TOP SONGS OF 1964 —
"I Want to Hold Your Hand," by the Beatles; "Hello, Dolly," by Louis Armstrong; "Oh, Pretty Woman," by Roy Orbison; "I Get Around," by The Beach Boys

RIGHT:
Whenever the noise subsided even slightly, the boys would do something adorable and the uproar would begin again.

146

Dozens of fans fainted in the crush. Fire warden Ed Jackson took one look and called for the portable oxygen units.

From a perch high in the stands, the Beckstead family from Winnipeg watched the remarkable scene through binoculars. "There was just a sea of people constantly trying to move forward," recalls Sharon, the family's ten-year-old Beatlemaniac. "Everyone was standing up to see what was going on, and I remember my father, who was still cranky from not getting enough sleep the night before, yelling at the people to sit down. I said, 'Dad, this isn't a symphony!' I was so embarrassed."

Big brother Jim decided to go down for a closer look and to take some photographs. "I got to within about twenty rows of the stage," he says. "All those people passing out and being carried off the field – it was horrific but fascinating at the same time. I took photos holding the camera over my head. But everything came out blurred."

Several times during the show the stadium's floodlights were switched on as a warning to the fans. Soon the situation became so critical that Errington and Brian Epstein summoned master of ceremonies Red Robinson to their side and told him that something had to be done to try to calm the audience down.

"Epstein was pretty worried by this point," Robinson remembers. "'Red,' he said, 'get on stage and stop the show. Tell those kids we won't continue if they don't calm down.'

"I started to argue. I didn't want to get in front of that hysterical audience. But Epstein practically shoved me onto the stage. As he did, Paul McCartney waved me off. Later, he told me that he thought that I thought the show was over. Then John Lennon saw me. 'Get the fuck off our stage!' he screamed at me. 'Nobody interrupts a Beatles performance!'"

Lennon's belligerent posture did little to endear him to Robinson, who had already decided he didn't like the young man during a brief meeting with the band in their trailer dressing room before the show. The other three all seemed like decent enough fellows, but Lennon "struck me as arrogant and pompous," Robinson says. "He appeared to consider himself far above his peers and seemed to enjoy the inevitable media putdowns more than the other three."

Over the roar of the crowd, Robinson attempted to explain his mission to Lennon. "John, they sent me up here," he yelled, pointing at Epstein and Errington. "Then Lennon relaxed a

LEFT:
"Even though they know they are not being heard they sing enthusiastically," noted the Toronto Daily Star.

FLASHBACK TO '64...
September 1 — Prime Minister Pearson and provincial premiers meet in Charlottetown to commemorate the Confederation conference of 1864.

RIGHT:
All hail the conquering heroes.

BELOW:
So dangerous was the situation at Empire Stadium that MC Red Robinson interrupted the show to plead for calm.

little. He said something like, 'Well, carry on then, old man.'"

Robinson's plea for calm went unheeded. "I remember how uncomfortable Red looked when he came out," says Della Darwin, the thirteen-year-old in the eleventh row. "He kept looking back over his shoulder. I don't think it occurred to any of us that they would actually stop the show."

The bedlam continued and the Beatles had no choice but to keep going. The situation was already dangerous enough. Who could guess what might happen if the group suddenly walked off the stage?

In Toronto, where the hysteria never threatened public safety but was just as sustained, the scene reminded one writer of a special kind of hell.

"Picture if you can the fitful light of a million flashbulbs striking on an endless sea of adolescents, and each female particle of that sea rending her hair and or garments, moaning and shrieking in every pitch the human voice is capable of, including probably those audible only to bats," wrote Ralph Hicklin of *The Globe and Mail.* "I kept expecting any minute that Cecil B. de Mille or his successor would yell 'Cut!' – and we'd have to start shooting The Revolt of Lucifer all over again...."

"A father might not even recognize his own daughter, that's how transformed those girls were," recalls disc jockey Duff Roman. "I very distinctly remember the hairs on my body standing on end. To see

that kind of giving-up of emotion for the first time was scary. This was a lot more primal than anything any of us had ever seen before, especially in WASP Toronto."

Bob Pennington, a dignified Englishman who covered the concerts for the old Toronto *Telegram*, complained of feeling "nauseated" by the scenes that surrounded him. Pennington found the situation in the press room at Maple Leaf Gardens, which police had turned into an emergency ambulance station, particularly appalling. "Where we once sat and talked of the Leafs, a wardful of females whose ages ranged from eight to the mid-twenties sobbed hysterically, or screamed in uncontrollable convulsions....

"These pitiful kids...had been conditioned by months of high-powered pressure, until these four Pied Pipers of our sick society would have stampeded them like demented sheep.

"If Niagara Falls had been outside, they would have followed John and George over in a barrel. Without question."

At one point Pennington turned to teenage television star Michele Finney, the special youth correspondent for the *Toronto Daily Star*. "Don't you think our society must be a little sick when this happens?" he asked her.

"No...no...they were absolutely marvellous," Finney said in defence of the Beatles.

At that moment the door burst open and another schoolgirl was brought kicking

153

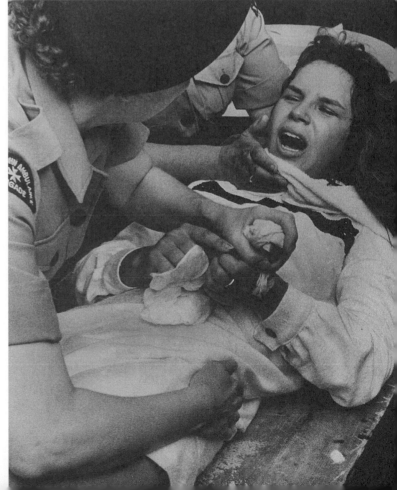

A Playlist for the Ages

THE FAB FOUR performed just twelve songs during each concert of the 1964 North American tour. They usually opened with "Twist and Shout" and closed with "Long Tall Sally." But, sometimes, they would drop "She Loves You" from the line-up and open with "I Saw Her Standing There," leaving "Twist and Shout" until the end. No matter the order, every last tune is indelibly etched in the memories of an entire generation.

Twist and Shout – Lennon acknowledged that he was only screaming the lyrics on this Isley Brothers number. It never failed to bring down the house at The Cavern in Liverpool.

You Can't Do That – Released as the B-side to "Can't Buy Me Love." Composed by Lennon:

"That's me doing Wilson Pickett."

All My Loving – Written by Paul: "It was the first song I ever wrote where I had the words before the music."

She Loves You – Lennon-McCartney. So tremendously popular that the Beatles rushed a German version – "Sie Liebt Dich" – into release.

Things We Said Today – Written by Paul while vacationing in the Bahamas. B-side to "A Hard Day's Night."

Roll Over Beethoven – George sings lead on this Chuck Berry composition.

Can't Buy Me Love – Lennon-McCartney, but mostly written by Paul. Five weeks atop the *Billboard* listing.

If I Fell – "That's my first attempt at a ballad proper," said author Lennon. B-side to "And I Love Her."

I Want to Hold Your Hand – Lennon-McCartney. Band's first North American smash. Held *Billboard*'s number-one position for seven weeks.

Boys – Ringo sings lead on this old Shirelles tune.

A Hard Day's Night – Movie title-song was written (by Lennon), arranged, rehearsed and recorded in just over twenty-four hours.

Long Tall Sally – Old Little Richard rave-up with Paul singing lead.

I Saw Her Standing There – Lennon-McCartney composition used as an alternate during the 1964 tour.

and screaming into the first-aid station. "I want Ringo, dear God, I want Ringo," she moaned.

Finney turned white, and said softly to Pennington, "I guess we are a little sick at that."

"The whole scene in the first-aid room really shook me," Michele says today. "I was very much a proper young lady and to see these young girls sobbing and their skirts flying up as they were subdued by the attendants – it all seemed so undignified."

Pennington continued ominously, "Some of us remember the first horror of the Nazi youth rallying. This was Toronto, 1964, and the same madness was afoot, produced by a vocal group the vast majority of the audience could hardly hear."

Pennington was far from the only adult who worried for the future of our youth after witnessing the effects of Beatlemania first-hand. The Vancouver *Province* dispatched University of British Columbia psychologist Dr. J. E. Ryan to the concert at Empire Stadium to get his analysis of the proceedings.

The good news was that Dr. Ryan believed that all teenagers needed an outlet for their "powerful emotions." Modern youth "are uncertain of everything," he said. "They have a tremendous amount of anxiety and in our society children are taught to repress it. They build up steam like a boiler and there has to be a form of release."

He just wished Canadian kids had found it in something other than the Beatles. Painting or writing or sports, Dr. Ryan suggested, would provide a much healthier release for the emotions. "However, it is better they go wild over the

According to at least one disapproving commentator, John Lennon and the other Beatles were the Pied Pipers of a sick society.

Beatles than become juvenile delinquents or become mentally ill."

A Vancouver psychologist believed that the Beatles provided a release for youthful emotions.

THE BEATLES REMAINED ON STAGE FOR JUST UNDER THIRTY minutes, which in those days was about the standard for rock 'n' roll headliners. They performed twelve songs in all, including most of their biggest hits: "She Loves You," "I Want to Hold Your Hand," "Can't Buy Me Love" and the title song from their smash movie *A Hard Day's Night.*

Predictably, most reviewers loathed their music and panned the concerts. But it should be noted that back then newspapers had not yet adopted the now-common practice of hiring hip young reporters to cover the rock scene. Most music critics of the day were at least middle-aged, with tastes that ran more to Puccini and Bach than to "Roll Over Beethoven," another hit included on the Beatles' playlist.

One of the few reviewers who found anything praiseworthy about the Beatles or their performance was Nathan Cohen, then widely regarded as the dean of Canadian critics. "They are energetic, good-natured and robustly masculine," Cohen wrote after watching the Beatles' first concert at Maple Leaf Gardens. "They have a sense of independence about them, of enjoying life to the full, which makes their appeal to the teenage generation easy to understand. On stage, they are strictly for the young teenager and the chances are they are going to remain popular for quite a while with them."

Far more typical was the reaction of William Littler of the Vancouver *Sun*, who dismissed the Beatles as nothing more than a passing fad. "…I perceived nothing that made them better or worse than any number of less ballyhooed groups, either as vocalists or instrumentalists. They sounded just as loud, just as monotonous, and just as unmusical….

"I do not know how it came and when it will go away. But go away the Beatle phenomenon will, and with it will go the Beatles. The day has yet to come. When it does, music lovers everywhere can rejoice – yeah, yeah, yeah."

A HALF-HOUR SHOW WHIZZED BY FOR FANATICS IN A TRANCE-LIKE state. Paul suddenly broke the spell by announcing their final number, "Long Tall Sally," the old Little Richard rave-up. The Beatles didn't do encores, so everyone knew this was it. The wailing and screaming scaled new heights – or depths, as most critics would have it.

When the last chords were struck, John, Paul, George and Ringo bent forward in a low bow. In a flash, they were off the stage and out of sight.

At the afternoon show in Toronto, hundreds of kids spontaneously surged towards the stage, only to be immediately checked by police and hustled to the exits. In Montreal, again at the end of the opening concert, a teenage girl took a running leap and tried to fling herself over the barrier surrounding the stage. Stunned young girls in the Vancouver audience huddled in small groups all over the stadium grounds, sobbing and embracing each other in consoling hugs.

This level of hysteria takes time to switch off. Outbursts of screaming continued long after the Beatles had gone. St. John

Many in the audiences were not yet out of grade school.

157

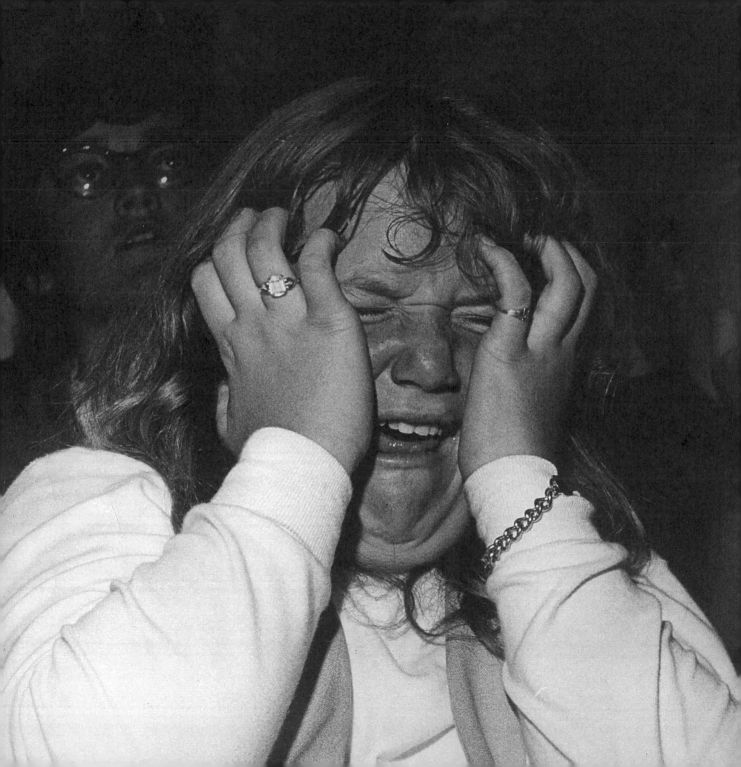

Ambulance attendants wandered through the stands, tending to girls too limp with exhaustion to move from their seats.

"That's one of my most vivid memories of the concert," says Torontonian Martin Black, "girls dropping like flies and then being picked up and carted off by the attendants. Where else would you ever see a sight like that? The whole show seemed unreal. But for me that was the most bizarre part."

Perhaps the strangest memory of all belongs to Eric Shapiro, who was twelve when he saw the evening show at the Forum. "This girl, who looked about sixteen, sat next to me," he says. "She was stone silent all through the opening acts. But once the Beatles came on, she suddenly went wild, completely nuts. She waved her arms and danced up and down in her seat. At first I hardly paid any attention, because I was concentrating on the Beatles. Then out of the corner of my eye I noticed that she was starting to take off her clothes. Her blouse came off first, then she started to wiggle out of her skirt. You can imagine how fascinating this was to a twelve-year-old boy. But even then I was torn between watching her and the stage. The girl was just starting to take off her bra when an attendant came along and hauled her away.

"I don't know what got into her," Shapiro adds. "Maybe she had heat prostration and just sort of lost it for a while. It was awfully hot in the arena. There's another thing I remember. When the attendant took her away, nobody but me even seemed to notice. Everyone was in his own little world, completely lost in what was happening on stage."

St. John Ambulance attendants treated more than one hundred cases of exhaustion, fainting, cuts, bruises and hysteria during the concerts in Toronto and Montreal. At Empire Stadium, the casualty count for the single show reached about one hundred and fifty. Soothing words, rest and cold

FLASHBACK TO '64...
September 27 — The Warren Commission report determines that Lee Harvey Oswald acted independently when he assassinated John F. Kennedy in Dallas, Texas, on November 22, 1963.

RIGHT:
*The Beatles make good their
getaway after the second show in
Toronto.*

compresses gently applied to head and shoulders quickly
returned most sufferers to their senses. Miraculously, there
wasn't a single serious injury.

It was St. John's busiest night ever in Vancouver.
Afterward, brigade supervisor R.D.E. Cook told his exhausted
team that they were now ready for anything, including nuclear
war. "You have had a good preview," he said, "of what you'd be
called upon to do in a full-scale emergency."

LESS THAN A MINUTE ELAPSED FROM THE TIME OF THE BEATLES'
final bow in Toronto until they were in the back of the paddy
wagon and cruising to the King Edward Hotel. Once again
police faked out the fans milling outside the Gardens, a crowd
more than four thousand strong. The bait was three police-
escorted limousines parked down the street at another entrance,
the same dodge used earlier in the day at the hotel.

Aides stocked the paddy wagon with towels for the Beatles
to mop off with and ice-cold bottles of Coke. By 11 p.m., the
four were back in the vice-regal suite and eager to get on with
the rest of the night's activities.

Waiting for photographer Boris Spremo outside the
Gardens was the young girl who had given him a tissue and
asked him to touch the Beatles with it. "I had her tissue for her,
although I can't honestly say I took the trouble to actually do
what she asked," Spremo says. "But I figured what she didn't
know couldn't hurt her. There were about fifteen girls gathered
around when I handed it to her. Then, like an idiot, I joked that
I had sat in Ringo's chair after the press conference. Holy
smoke! Those girls were on me like a pack of animals. They
started screaming and tearing at my pants, trying to pull them
off. They chased me all the way down Church Street to where
my car was parked. I could have gotten killed."

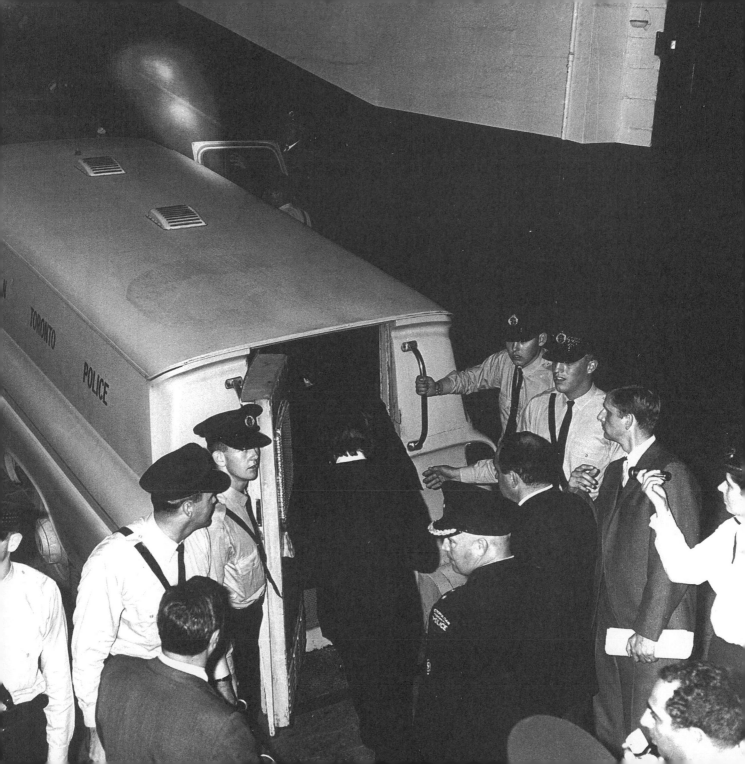

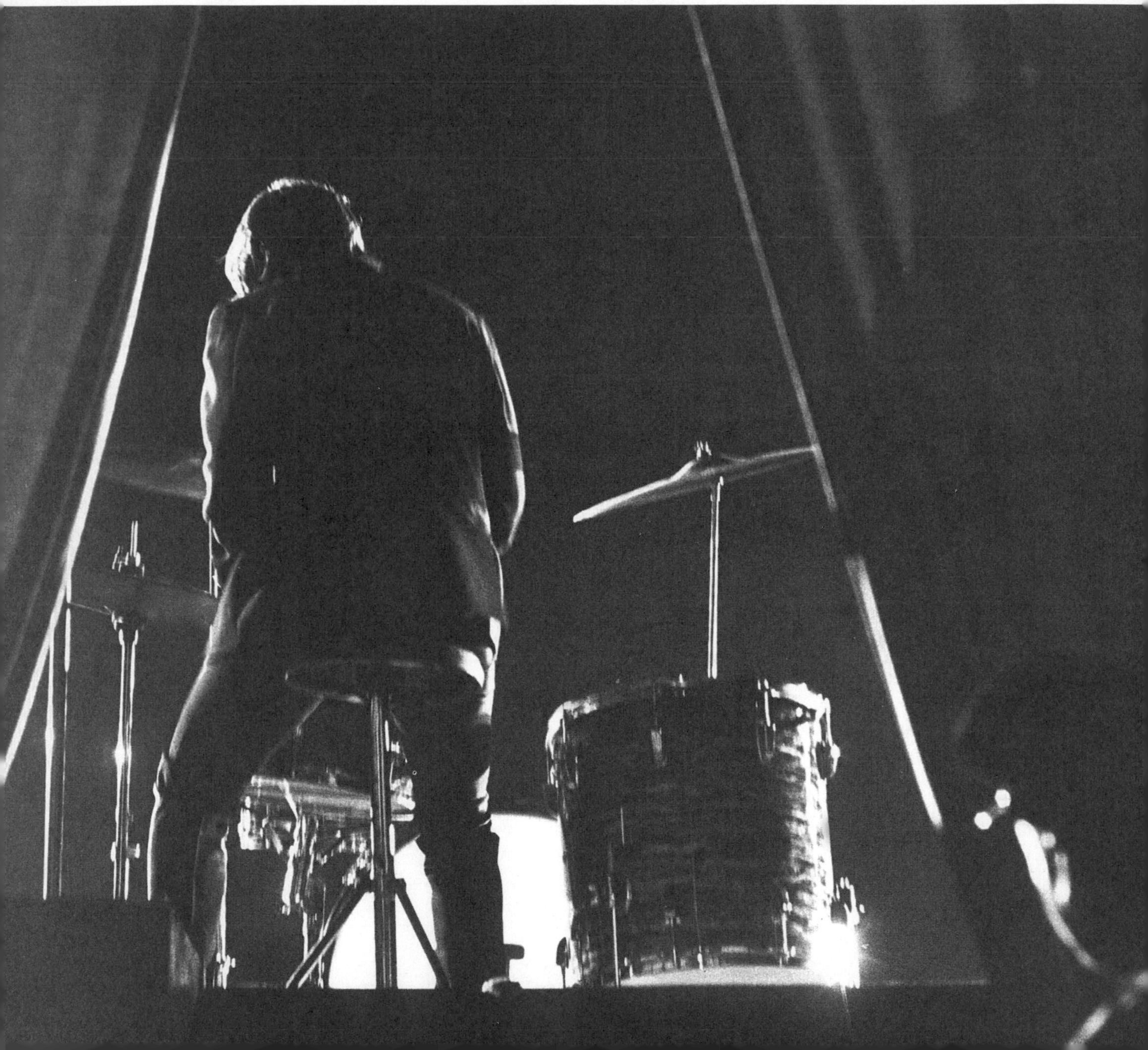

Outside the Montreal Forum's St. Luke Street entrance, three limousines stood ready for the Beatles' getaway. But the chauffeur, possibly still a little jittery after being berated by George Harrison for speeding during the ride into town, put the wrong key into the ignition, then dropped the chain. Panicked by the prospect of even the slightest delay, police had already started moving the Beatles to another car when he finally got the engine running. Doors slammed and the convoy set off. The remainder of the drive to the airport proceeded without incident.

At Vancouver's Empire Stadium, police had cleared a path beyond the southeast gate. The heavy door swung open and the Beatles' motorcycle escort roared through. One young tough tossed a bicycle in front of the lead motorcycle in an attempt to foil the escape. The convoy swerved around it without losing speed. At the airport, the Beatles' rented Electra stood ready for a flight to Los Angeles.

The next night at a packed Hollywood Bowl, they would do it all over again. "Go ahead and let yourselves go," John Lennon urged the crowd. "It's not our place anyway."

LEFT:
At each concert the loudest cheers were reserved for Ringo.

Hello, Goodbye *Chapter 6*

Gesture of an ebullient teenager marks arrival of the mop-haired quartet

Here they are: George, Ringo, John, Paul

Hurricane-Bound Beatles Find Montreal 'A Breeze'

Quartet Faced Well-Controlled Teenage Audience Here

The hurricane-bound Beatles found Montreal a
real breeze after they touched down here yesterday
on their North American tour.

Mop-topped George, John, Ringo and Paul were
met with maximum enthusiasm but minimum hysteria
in two Forum shows during the eight hours they
spent here before they flew off to Jacksonville, Fla.,
and a possible encounter with Hurricane Dora.

Behind them they left 12 teenaged girls treated for
hysteria and minor cuts and bruises; a policeman
recuperating from a bit-
ten thumb; 500 tired,
rain - soaked Montreal
policemen and a happy
relieved staff at Montreal
International Airport in
Dorval.

Also behind they left
21,000 cheering, scream-
ing, swooning fans; 22
songs; and a few gems of
Beatlemania.

Sample:
Question: What do the
Beatles do when th...

By Terry Haig and Al Palmer

ed up in a hotel room between
shows?

Answer: "We ice skate."
(Yeah, Yeah, Yeah.)

After their chartered plane
took off from Dorval at 11.46
p.m. last night it was dis...
...they also had left
behind the outsized Ookpik...

PRECEDING PAGES:
*Fans spell out their devotion to
Paul McCartney at the Montreal
airport.*

SAFE AGAIN IN THEIR HOTEL LAIR, the Beatles hosted
a party into the wee hours after the Toronto concerts.
Record executives, disc jockeys and reporters crowded
into the King Edward's vice-regal suite drinking up the free
booze and trying hard to catch the boys' attention.

In the streets below, two thousand fans, about half the
number of the night before, stood a noisy watch. "Really, just
two thousand? I was in their suite that night and it sounded like
there were ten times that many outside," recalls Bob Burns, the
Winnipeg dance-show host who had been the first to interview
the Beatles in Canada. "I remember going to one of the windows
and pulling it open. The kids below were singing the lyrics from
'I Should Have Known Better.' It was just this massive, unison
chorus. You could hear it like it was right in the room."

Malaysia...
Gurkha Troops Hunt Indonesians
— Tough little British Gurkha troops,
...into the country 'de Tues...
Troops Fly In

Under Shipping A
Launched In Cra

Burns had journeyed east for a second interview with the Beatles, this time for a documentary on the Toronto concerts being prepared by his TV station. His brief chat with them on the tarmac at Winnipeg International Airport had given him only an admittedly superficial impression of their personalities. The Beatle Burns liked best during that first encounter was Ringo, the only one who took his questions seriously. Paul and George, from what he could tell, conformed to their public images of baby-faced charmer and enigmatic dreamer.

This lucky girl gets a personal goodbye from Paul, John and Ringo at Toronto International Airport, where the lads playfully indulged the crowd.

Like Red Robinson in Vancouver, Burns found John Lennon the least agreeable of the four. "He seemed rude and arrogant, somewhere in a zone all his own." But after interviewing John and the others earlier in the day at Maple Leaf Gardens, and then talking to him briefly at the party in their suite, Burns began to change his opinion. He would turn around completely about Lennon three years later when the two met up again in Swinging London. By

JOHN LENNON RELAXES AT HOTEL
Wearing gay gift pyjamas from admirer

that time Burns had added the management of the rising Canadian rock band The Guess Who to his portfolio.

"I bumped into John at the Bag O' Nails, a very trendy club down in Soho where all the top pop stars hung out. We started talking and then he drove me back to my hotel in that famous Rolls-Royce he had had painted in psychedelic colours. That's when I really learned to appreciate John Lennon. I found him absolutely brilliant, with a mind like a steel trap. The man was also very witty, but you had to understand his wit to appreciate it. Naturally, I had no way of knowing any of this when we first met."

John, the Beatle who would form the closest ties to Canada in the coming years, was in especially good form the night of the party. After Brian Epstein and aides cleared most of the guests out of the suite, Lennon playfully modelled a garish red-and-black-striped pyjama set sent in by a fan. He completed the ensemble with a jaunty top hat, which he claimed to sleep in.

John still had the outfit on a little later when Miss Canada, Mary Lou Farrell, was ushered into the Beatles' suite. The stunning twenty-one-year-old Newfoundlander spent a convivial hour or so just as she might have with friends back home on The Rock – drinking soda pop and munching on toast. "I'm not a Beatles fan or anything," she confessed later. "I've never bought their records. But they're just like my three brothers at home."

Then the Beatles, ciggies and Scotch-and-Cokes at hand, settled in for a game of poker, a shared passion that occupied countless hours of down time during the run of the tour. Each played his cards with the confidence of knowing that any losses would be more than offset by a share of the $93,000 cheque

169

ABOVE:
Wearing a garish pyjama set sent by a fan, John posed for photographers back at the hotel after the Toronto concerts.

LEFT:
Ten minutes after the Beatles' plane took off from the Toronto airport, heartsick girls still clung to the wire fence.

FLASHBACK TO '64...
October 10 — Separatists demonstrate during the visit of Queen Elizabeth and Prince Philip to Quebec City.

received earlier in the evening from Maple Leaf Gardens.

At about 1:30 a.m., Toronto mayor Phil Givens and his wife, who had attended another function at the King Edward, knocked on the Beatles' door, hoping to pay their respects. According to His Worship, they received an exceedingly "rude and offensive" reception from an unidentified blonde woman who answered the door.

Toronto mayor Phil Givens complained that he was rudely rebuffed at the Beatles' door.

170

"We told her umpteen times I was the mayor of Toronto," Givens angrily recounted, "but she wouldn't even have the courtesy to take my card in to them. Then she said, 'Two of them are asleep and two of them are with relatives. Nobody gets in,' and slammed the door in my face."

The next day, the blonde, who turned out to be Bess Coleman, a Beatles aide, said that if the mayor had phoned when the Beatles arrived in Toronto, she would have happily arranged a meeting at a more appropriate hour. "It was a case of two very tired boys being in bed, and George Harrison had relatives visiting.

"I was not rude and I'm sorry that the mayor thought me offensive," Coleman concluded tartly.

Just as she said, George Harrison was preoccupied with visits from family during his stay in Toronto. His sister Louise, who had emigrated to the United States, drove in with her husband and two children from their home in Illinois. "He looked tired and he needed a rest," she said, full of concern after meeting with George that morning.

Many people close to the Beatles in those days wrote instant memoirs or found some other way to cash in on the connection. Louise Harrison hosted a daily sixty-second radio spot for several stations in Canada and the United States. "Not for the money, though," she insisted. "It's mainly to answer all the false and sullied stories that sometimes get circulated."

Also on hand was George's uncle Edmund French, a trucking supervisor who made his home in Toronto. He had last seen his nephew eleven years before, when he had left Liverpool. Edmund thought some of the Beatles' tunes "very nice" and remembered that "George always did like to play the guitar."

Considerably less impressed by George's success was his thirteen-year-old cousin Gregory, Edmund's son. "They're all right, I guess," he shrugged when asked about the Beatles earlier in the day. He entertained himself during the visit by poking his head out a window of the suite to incite the crowd in the street. Even after watching Uncle George and his mates perform live for the first time, Gregory's verdict hadn't changed. "They're all right, I guess," he shrugged again, apparently still the only teenager in Toronto unmoved by the Beatles' magic.

THINGS HAD QUIETED DOWN OUTSIDE THE King Edward Hotel by the next morning.

Fans kept a watchful vigil outside the King Edward Hotel.

RIGHT:
Police hold back the crowd surrounding the hotel.

Only a few hundred kids skipped off the first day of school for the Beatles' checkout. Once again police employed a flying wedge, a technique they had had ample opportunity to perfect during the course of the weekend, to clear a path to the limousines. "But while on Monday a mighty shriek from thousands of teenage throats rose in the air, yesterday's ovations were but a thin wail," noted *The Globe and Mail* the next day. Mention was also made that the Beatles' police escort on the way out of town was no larger than that given Prime Minister Lester Pearson whenever he visited Toronto.

The King Edward, the only Canadian hotel ever to host all four Beatles, would see the band twice more. But for the moment a collective sigh of relief greeted their departure. "I've seen everything," said a weary Joseph F. Downey, the resident manager. "But the Beatles were incredible."

About three hundred fans saw them off at the airport. Before boarding the Electra for the short flight to Montreal, John, Paul and Ringo approached the fence alongside the tarmac to wave and shout at the faithful. George, ordinarily the most accommodating of the four, immediately entered the plane and for reasons unknown refused to come out.

With no need to worry about their personal safety, the three remaining Beatles playfully indulged the relative handful of fans and officials on the scene for almost fifteen minutes before takeoff. Paul took photos of the crowd and the police, and even of the photographers taking photos of him. The Beatles also politely thanked the cops who had protected them during their visit.

"Don't go Ringo!" "Don't let them go," pleaded the kids on the other side of the fence. Ten minutes after the plane took off, heartsick girls still clung like mosquitoes to the wire mesh.

Montreal fans should have been half so lucky. That night

174

at the airport in Dorval, tired out after the two concerts and anxious to escape Montreal after the threat to Ringo, the boys didn't make even the slightest effort to accommodate the three hundred fans standing in drizzling rain on the observation deck. The crowd screamed itself hoarse waiting for a sign of their affection. Off-duty airport personnel and ground hostesses gathered under the cover of the plane's wings, hoping for a glimpse of them. But not as much as a curtain moved the entire length of the aircraft.

Nervous flyers all, especially after the psychic's prediction that the Electra would crash sometime during the tour, the Beatles may have been preoccupied by the perils of the journey ahead. Their flight to Jacksonville, Florida, where they had a gig at the Gator Bowl, took them into the path of Hurricane Dora. Thousands were fleeing their homes as tides as much as

In June of 1965, word came from Buckingham Palace that the Beatles would each receive the MBE – "Membership of the Most Excellent Order of the British Empire."

ten feet above normal battered the Florida coast. President Lyndon Johnson declared Jacksonville a disaster area.

Although at least nine thousand ticket-holders found it impossible to make their way to the Gator Bowl, the concert went on as scheduled Friday night. The Beatles performed on a stage lashed by forty-mile-an-hour winds. Poor Ringo had to have his drums nailed down to keep them from blowing away.

AFTER PLAYING TO MORE THAN 350,000 FANS, THE FAB FOUR'S first North American tour ended September 20 in New York. *Variety*, the show business bible, estimated that the proceeds from their recordings, movie and personal appearances earned the Beatles at least $50 million on this side of the Atlantic alone in 1964. (But, remember, one of them joked at the Vancouver press conference, that's not so much when you split it four ways.)

A scene from the Beatles' second movie, Help!

The next months saw the Beatles complete the filming of their second movie, *Help!,* for which they diligently prepared by studying the Marx Brothers' classic, *Duck Soup.* Unfortunately, the final result was an incomprehensible farce despised by the band and panned by critics. The best thing in it was the title song, which shot to number one.

In June of 1965, Buckingham Palace announced that the Beatles, whose recordings had injected millions of pounds into the Exchequer, would each receive the MBE – "Membership of the Most Excellent Order of the British Empire."

"I thought you had to drive tanks and

175

win wars to get the MBE," John said.

"I'll keep it to dust when I'm old," added Ringo.

Several MBE-holders returned their decorations rather than share the honour with, as an outraged naval hero phrased it, "a gang of nincompoops." John recalled that on the day of their investiture, the Beatles celebrated by smoking a marijuana joint in a Buckingham Palace washroom. George has said that Lennon's memory was faulty, that they smoked nothing stronger than a cigarette. "I was too stoned to remember," shrugged Ringo.

"We've played Frisco's Cow Palace but never one like this," said Paul McCartney of the royal digs. "It's a keen pad."

And the Queen? "She was like a mum to us," he said.

On August 13, 1965, the Beatles kicked off another North American tour with a spectacularly successful performance at New York's Shea Stadium. The evening set new rock-concert records for the largest attendance (55,600), for the largest gross revenue ($304,000) and for the largest fee ever paid to a headline act ($160,000).

They hit Toronto, the only Canadian stop on the ten-city tour, August 17, for a pair of sold-out shows at Maple Leaf Gardens. On a hot and muggy day, fans at the matinee sweated out a ninety-minute delay when the Beatles' plane was slowed by storms. The fearsome heat in the building gave rise to the spurious rumour (still

LEFT:
Fans welcome their heroes back to Canada in the summer of 1965.

BELOW:
The Beatles disembark at the airport in Toronto, the band's only Canadian stop of the 1965 summer tour.

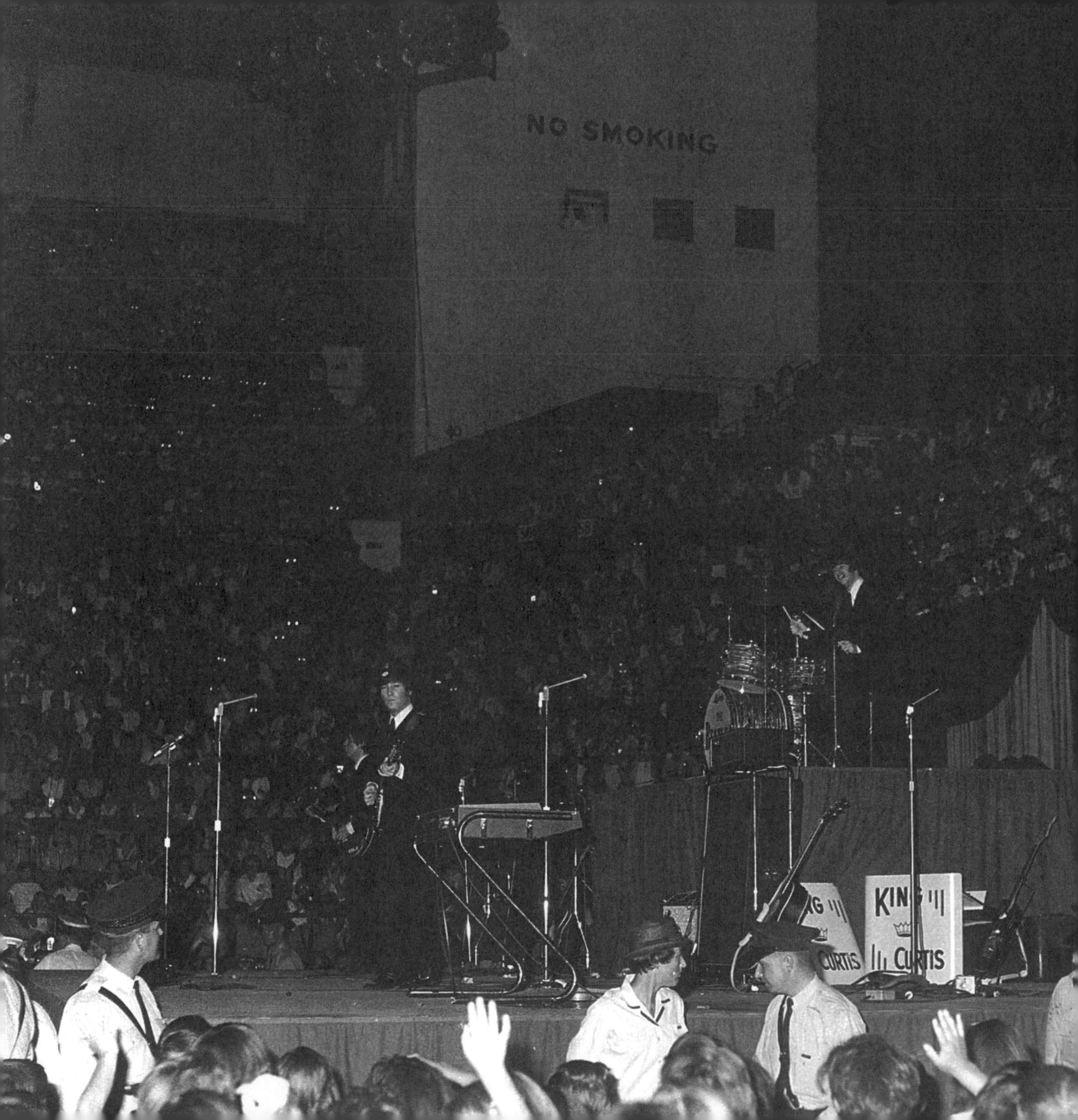
NO SMOKING
KING CURTIS
KING CURTIS

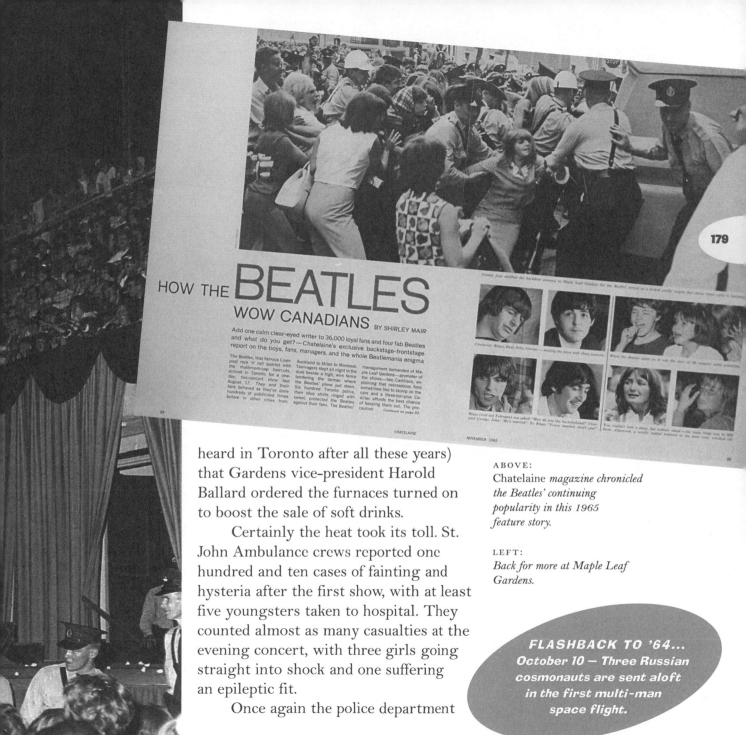

heard in Toronto after all these years) that Gardens vice-president Harold Ballard ordered the furnaces turned on to boost the sale of soft drinks.

Certainly the heat took its toll. St. John Ambulance crews reported one hundred and ten cases of fainting and hysteria after the first show, with at least five youngsters taken to hospital. They counted almost as many casualties at the evening concert, with three girls going straight into shock and one suffering an epileptic fit.

Once again the police department

ABOVE:
Chatelaine magazine chronicled the Beatles' continuing popularity in this 1965 feature story.

LEFT:
Back for more at Maple Leaf Gardens.

FLASHBACK TO '64...
October 10 — Three Russian cosmonauts are sent aloft in the first multi-man space flight.

mustered all its forces to control the crowds at the Gardens and outside the King Edward Hotel, where the Beatles spent the night. But while six hundred men in blue massed downtown, law and order took a beating elsewhere in the city. Criminals seized the opportunity to rob a bank and a suburban trust company. The administration of justice at the city's courts also slowed to a crawl.

Though it came close, the general hysteria in Toronto and elsewhere didn't quite match that of the previous summer. And by their next visit a year later, there could no longer be any doubt about it: Beatlemania was on the decline. Few concerts on the 1966 North American summer tour played to capacity audiences, including the two shows at Maple Leaf Gardens (once again Toronto was the only Canadian stop). Fans were finally refusing to pay good money to see the Fab Four deliver an inaudible, too often half-hearted performance a scant half-hour long. Three thousand seats went unsold at the Gardens for the afternoon performance; one thousand for the evening show. A mere four hundred fans turned out at the airport to welcome the lads back to Hogtown.

At any rate, by this point John, Paul, George and Ringo had had more than their fill of touring. "Beatles concerts are

FAR LEFT AND BELOW:
*More than two hundred cases of
fainting and hysteria were
reported during the Toronto
shows in 1965.*

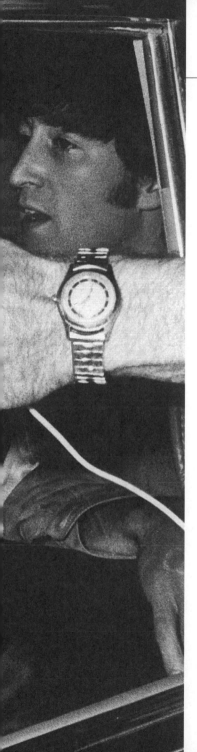

nothing to do with music any more," John said in disgust. "They're just bloody tribal rites."

Lennon was the centre of a controversy that simmered the length of the tour. Months before an interviewer had quoted him as saying: "We're more popular than Jesus now. I don't know which will go first – rock 'n' roll or Christianity." When an American teen magazine picked up the story, the outcry was so great that twenty American and several Canadian radio stations banned Beatles records. Some cities in the Bible Belt held massive bonfires, inviting youngsters to stoke the flames with their Beatles albums and paraphernalia.

John, though expressing puzzlement at the uproar, apologized for his statements at the start of the tour. A week later during the ritual press conference in Toronto, he insisted that his comments had been taken out of context. Lennon added that the only people who took offence were middle-aged DJs and a few others "we don't care about anyway."

The Beatles planned a full-time retreat to the sanctuary of the recording studio, where their genius would soon reach its full flower. Already many of their recordings were too musically intricate to successfully duplicate on

LEFT:
"We're glad to be back in Toronto," said Paul McCartney in 1966. But, in truth, the Beatles were tiring of life on the road.

183

TOP NEW TV SHOWS OF 1964 — "Gilligan's Island"; "Gomer Pyle USMC"; "The Munsters"; "The Man from U.N.C.L.E."; "Flipper"; "The Addams Family"; "Bewitched"; "Voyage to the Bottom of the Sea."

stage, even if their fans would stop screaming long enough to listen. And so their tour-ending concert at San Francisco's Candlestick Park on August 29, 1966, proved to be the band's last ever. After more than fourteen hundred live appearances, they finished with "Long Tall Sally," bowed in unison and fled one final time into the safety of a waiting armoured van.

THE MANIA WAS OVER — BUT THE INFLUENCE OF THE BEATLES has never waned. When they adopted garish Carnaby Street outfits, everyone began to dress and strut the streets like peacocks. They experimented with drugs and an entire generation turned on. They spoke out against war and the peace movement gained new momentum. The Beatles steered millions on a voyage of self-discovery that for many has continued into middle age and beyond.

In the spring of 1967, they released the epochal *Sgt. Pepper's Lonely Hearts Club Band*, which was all radios and stereos seemed to play during the following "Summer of Love." For Canadians, giddily celebrating the nation's centennial at Expo 67, only Bobby Gimby's treacly but maddeningly catchy "Canada" equalled *Sgt. Pepper's* impact.

The Beatles kept pushing the boundaries. They studied in India with the Maharishi Mahesh Yogi and embarked with a midget, a fat lady, a music-hall comedian and other unique friends on a filmed bus trip through Britain they called a "Magical Mystery Tour." And through it all they kept spinning out the

The jacket cover for Sgt. Pepper's Lonely Hearts Club Band, *the only album radios seemed to play during the summer of 1967.*

hits: "Penny Lane," "Strawberry Fields" and "All You Need Is Love" in 1967; "Hey Jude" and "Hello, Goodbye" in 1968; and "Get Back" and "Come Together" in 1969.

John Lennon, especially, yearned to branch out in new directions. In 1968 he left his wife, Cynthia, for the Japanese-born performance artist Yoko Ono. The two immediately became an inseparable unit Lennon referred to as "johnandyoko." For seven days in March of 1969, they conducted a bed-in for peace at the Amsterdam Hilton. "What we're really doing," John said, "is sending out a message to the world, mainly to the youth, to anybody who is interested in protesting for peace or protesting any form of violence."

After marrying in Gibraltar later that spring, they brought their peace campaign to Canada, where they encamped at Montreal's Queen Elizabeth Hotel from May 26 to June 2. In

The boys in full Sgt. Pepper's regalia. Note the Ontario Provincial Police patch on Paul's sleeve, which was sent to him by a Canadian fan.

The Beatles kept churning out the hits for the remainder of the 1960s. This unique B-flat trumpet (seen during an auction at Sotheby's in 1987) was used in the recording of "Penny Lane," which topped the charts in 1967.

truth, they had hoped to conduct this second bed-in in the United States, but John's visa application was rejected because of a conviction in Britain the year before for possession of hashish.

No matter. Montreal's close proximity to the U.S. border ensured that their message saturated the media of a nation then embroiled in a painful debate over its involvement in the Vietnam War. An average of one hundred and fifty journalists squeezed into their hotel room every day. John and Yoko called more than three hundred U.S. radio stations to talk peace.

The highlight of the couple's Montreal stay was the recording of "Give Peace a Chance," which immediately became both an anthem and a slogan for the anti-war movement. From his bed, Lennon strummed guitar and sang lead for an eclectic chorus that included LSD guru Timothy Leary, comedian and activist Tommy Smothers, bell-ringing, bald-headed followers of the Canadian chapter of the Radha Krishna Temple, a rabbi and a priest.

Canada drew John and Yoko back twice more in 1969. They first returned Saturday, September 13, when the newly formed Plastic Ono Band made its world debut during a rock 'n' roll revival at Toronto's Varsity Stadium. Lennon accepted his invitation to attend just thirty-six hours before the gates opened. On the

LEFT:
John Lennon and Yoko Ono during their bed-in for peace at Montreal's Queen Elizabeth Hotel in 1969.

BELOW:
Toronto rabbi Abraham Feinberg visited John and Yoko in their hotel room while the couple rehearsed the anti-war anthem "Give Peace a Chance."

strength of his appearance, the promoters sold ten thousand tickets the day of the concert. Included on the bill were Little Richard, Chuck Berry, Jerry Lee Lewis, Fats Domino, Bo Diddley, as well as contemporary acts The Doors and Alice Cooper.

By now Lennon had told the other Beatles of his intention to quit the band and pursue a solo career. Open conflict had recently flared between John and Paul McCartney over the group's musical direction. Yoko's constant presence in the recording studio and her influence over John also annoyed and distracted the other Beatles. But because of contractual obligations, the break-up could not yet be made public.

Having hastily assembled a supporting band that included guitarist Eric Clapton, Lennon and the others rehearsed on the flight to Toronto from London. So nervous that he vomited before going on stage, John ripped through a set that included "Blue Suede Shoes," "Money (That's What I Want)," "Dizzy Miss Lizzie" and his own compositions "Yer Blues" and "Cold Turkey." Before his final number, "Give Peace a Chance," the audience of twenty-seven thousand stood en masse and made the two-fingered V-for-peace sign.

For a long perfect moment the world seemed as one. But John broke the spell by announcing that it was Yoko's turn at the microphone. "She's gonna do her thing all over you," he promised.

Yoko, who until that point had spent her time on stage inside a large white bag, began braying in a high-pitched wail, accompanied only by amplifier feedback. On and on it went until many in the audience began to boo. According to one reporter on the scene, "Yoko's keening drove at least five acid

FAR LEFT:
Yoko Ono and John Lennon onstage in Toronto during a 1969 rock 'n' roll revival.

BELOW:
These were years of personal and musical experimentation for the Beatles. Here George, in the company of actress Rita Tushingham, strums a sitar during a recording session in Bombay.

189

John and Yoko Meet the Media Guru

LEADERSHIP, public image, even the threat of Quebec separation. According to Canada's famed communication theorist Dr. Marshall McLuhan, our politicians could improve their performance on all these issues by emulating the Beatles.

"The Beatles," McLuhan said, "tell us they want to 'hold our hand' and in expressing this wish they may appear to come close to the popular image of the politician. There is about them, however, something that is new and radical. They really do speak with the authority of the electronic age."

McLuhan made his comments to a Conservative Party conference in Fredericton on September 9, 1964, just after the band's last Canadian stop of the first North American tour. The Fab Four, he continued, "have invented an image in which the relation of the individual and a group has been refocussed for our time."

McLuhan's audience at the conference responded with a collective, "Huh?" But, then, the University of Toronto professor always left a lot of people wondering what the heck he was talking about.

Five years later, McLuhlan would meet with John Lennon and Yoko Ono when they dropped into his office during a visit to Toronto to promote their proposed Music and Peace Conference of the World. According to Lennon biographer Albert Goldman, John, regarded as the most intellectual of the Beatles, held his own in a rapid-fire give-and-take with the media guru.

"Language is a form of organized stutter," McLuhan started in. "Literally, you chop your sounds up into bits in order to talk. Now, when you sing, you don't stutter, so singing is a way of stretching language into long, harmonious patterns and cycles. How do you think about language in songs?"

Without missing a beat, Lennon replied: "Language and song to me, apart from being pure vibrations, is just like trying to describe a dream. And because we don't have telepathy, we try and describe the dream to each other, to verify to each other what we know, what we believe to be inside each other. And the stuttering is right — because we can't say it. No matter how you say it, it's never how you want to say it."

Duly impressed, Dr. McLuhan saw the Lennons out with the parting words, "These portals have been honoured by your presence."

Dr. Marshall McLuhan.

heads to seek help for their beleaguered brains."

John Lennon's performance, though at times ragged, thrilled the audience. Even Yoko expressed satisfaction with her reception. "In any concert, we hope to get a strong reaction," she said. "The booing? Well, what we're doing – well, it's a start. You don't expect something new to be accepted overnight."

John and Yoko talked peace with Prime Minister Pierre Trudeau during a visit to Canada in December, 1969.

191

The world's most famous couple was developing a sincere fondness for Canada. "The press in Canada gives us a chance," Lennon enthused that December. "They treat us as human beings, which is a pleasant change. It seems that we get more smiles and genuine help from Canada than anywhere else – that's why we're here."

They came back this time to lay the groundwork for the Music and Peace Conference of the World, a mammoth festival planned for the next summer at Mosport, a car-racing track on a well-wooded site about forty miles from Toronto. John said the festival was designed for "musicians, poets, artists to do their thing for peace." He and the other organizers (including some of the same people who had bankrolled the rock 'n' roll revival) hoped to attract as many as a million people to the festival with a line-up that would include the biggest names in rock. The event was to be beamed via satellite to television sets around the world. Lennon even hoped to lure Elvis Presley north to perform alongside him in a grand finale.

From the Toronto-area estate of singer Rompin' Ronnie Hawkins, John and Yoko sallied forth to spread their peace message and arrange the details

LEFT:
While staying at a farm near Toronto owned by singer Rompin' Ronnie Hawkins, the Lennons enjoyed their first snowmobile ride.

FLASHBACK TO '64...
December 15 — The House of Commons votes 163 to 78 for a Canadian flag with a red maple leaf on a white background flanked by vertical red bars.

of the festival. On Saturday, December 20, they met with Prime Minister Pierre Trudeau at his office in Ottawa. They discussed John's poetry and his life as a Beatle, the generation gap and their peace efforts. Trudeau, attentive and at his most charming, said they gave him renewed hope for the future of the world's youth and about the prospects for peace.

John and Yoko practically gushed the prime minister's praises when they emerged after almost an hour. "If all politicians were like Mr. Trudeau," Lennon said, "there would be world peace. You don't know how lucky you are in Canada."

Added Yoko, "We got a great incentive by just meeting him and seeing that there are such people as him in the Establishment." She agreed with John that the prime minister was one of the beautiful people – "yes, more beautiful than we expected."

Everything seemed possible in those heady last days of the sixties. After their appointment with Trudeau, the couple dashed off to see Minister of Health John Munro. Asked what it was about, Lennon answered: "To keep the festival healthy, man."

But, as history records, the Music and Peace Conference of the World never happened. Elvis Presley didn't even bother to answer Lennon's phone calls. The logistical planning for such a massive gathering proved a nightmare. After flying home to London for Christmas, John and Yoko quickly lost enthusiasm for the project and pursued other interests.

On Friday, April 10, 1970, confirmation came from London that the Beatles, the most popular band in the history of the world, had officially parted company.

"I used to think of them as the sparkly people. Everything about the Beatles seemed magical," says Robin Timmerman, who camped out in the cold and rain to be first in line for tickets at Maple Leaf Gardens. "It was a very optimistic and exciting time. I just wanted to be part of it all."

Cynthia Good, the girl in the "Yeah, Yeah, Yeah" sweater who wandered the hallways of the King Edward Hotel kissing doorknobs, says: "I knew even at that age that the Beatles were an important part of history. I felt lucky to be alive for it."

"I just admired them so much – and I still do," says Sharon Beckstead, the Winnipegger unexpectedly plunked down in the middle of Beatlemania during a family vacation in Vancouver. "I still remember the sensation I caused when I got back to

The Beatles very near the end.

school. 'What did you do on your summer vacation?' 'Well, I saw the Beatles.'"

Eric Twiname, the musician from Montreal who jilted Buddy Holly for the Beatles, still has his perfectly preserved souvenir programme. "'My little baby,' I call it. I pull it out every now and again to remember the greatest concert I ever saw in my life."

None too surprisingly, the fanatical devotion of Edith Manea, the Beatle-Manea twin, has also survived the passing years. She saw the Fab Four perform live a total of seven times – at four more concerts in Toronto (including both the matinee and evening shows in 1965 and 1966), and twice in Detroit, after hitch-hiking there with her sister and a girlfriend.

"The Beatles were such a huge part of my life," Edith says. "When I heard the news that they had broken up, I felt as if my parents had told me they were getting a divorce."

She still gets goosebumps whenever she hears the old songs. "I know every lyric to every Beatles recording. I grew up with those songs. Each one brings back a certain memory or a feeling.

"I have two great kids, I'm happily married, I think I've got a great life," the Beatle-Manea twin continues. "But those days will always be special. I still think of them as the best times of all."

Acknowledgements

At least as much as the words that tell the story, the success of a book such as this depends on the unique talents of its art director. I am deeply indebted to Martin Gould of Penguin Books Canada, who allowed himself to be persuaded to undertake the project and then saw it through a lengthy incubation with unflagging patience and good humour. There's no one with whom I would have rather worked or who I think could have done a better job.

Among the many other people who assisted in the creation of *Our Hearts Went Boom*, a special thank you has to go to Peter Miniaci, the owner of Toronto's Beatlemania Shoppe. Peter opened his files to give me the telephone numbers of many of the Beatlemaniacs quoted on these pages. He also generously supplied many of the collectibles for photographing.

Another who provided tremendous help was research assistant Chris Matto. His keen eye uncovered several colourful bits of Beatles lore that I might otherwise have missed.

There are still others to thank: C.G. O'Brien at radio station CHUM in Toronto; noted Beatles memorabilia collector Andrew Croft; former Beatles fan club president Trudy Medcalf, who is known these days by her married name of Litster; Phil Rogers of CKY-TV in Winnipeg; Vancouver radio personality Red Robinson; Edith Manea, one half of Toronto's Beatle-Manea twins, who now goes by her married name of Ippolito; and musicologist Rob

Bowman. Each of them offered encouragement and insights, and kindly loaned us archival material.

I would also like to express my gratitude to copy editor Mary Adachi, who is both a pleasure to work with and a consummate pro.

No book about the Beatles can possibly be completed without building on the work of the journalists and authors who have tackled the subject before. During the course of my research, I spent many happy hours reading the accounts of the band's invasion of Canada that appeared in the daily newspapers of Vancouver, Winnipeg, Toronto and Montreal.

I also consulted about two dozen of the many books written about the Beatles. Of these, several titles proved particularly helpful: *The Complete Beatles Chronicle* by Mark Lewisohn (Harmony Books, 1992); *Beatlesongs* by William J. Dowlding (Fireside, 1989); *Shout: The Beatles in Their Generation* by Philip Norman (MJF Books, 1991); *The Lives of John Lennon* by Albert Goldman (William Morrow, 1988); *Beatles '64, A Hard Day's Night in America* – text by A. J. S. Rayl, photographs by Curt Gunther (Doubleday, 1989); and *How They Became the Beatles: A Definitive History of the Early Years, 1960-64* by Gareth L. Pawlowski (E. P. Dutton, 1989).

Finally, a heartfelt note of appreciation to my editor and publisher, Cynthia Good of Penguin Books Canada. No author could possibly hope for a more enthusiastic mentor than the fab bird in the second row wearing the "Yeah, Yeah, Yeah" sweater.

Photo Credits

Jim Beckstead private collection: 39, 55, 59, 140 (bottom left); Canapress: ii, 5 (bottom), 6, 10, 35, 47–49, 51, 69–70, 102, 174, 185–86, 187 (bottom), 189, 191–93, 195; CKY-TV: 45–46; *The Globe and Mail*: 84, 88–91, 111, 129, 188, 190; Cynthia Good private collection: 86; Martin Gould: 5 (top), 14–15, 17, 52, 60, 82, 87, 104, 114–15, 130, 142; Graphic Artists: 4, 19–21, 25, 31, 74, 76, 78, 80, 94, 100–101, 110, 113, 119, 123, 128, 131–33, 136–37, 146–49, 151, 154, 156–57, 161–63, 178–79, 181, 197; Edith Ippolito private collection: 27 (right), 79, 139; Trudy Medcalf private collection: 13, 26–27, 109; *Montreal Gazette*: 158, 164–65, 187 (top); Pacific Press Ltd.: 42–43, 124–27, 134–135, 138, 140–41, 152; Red Robinson private collection: 56–57, 103, 143, 150, 155; *Toronto Star* Syndicate: 22–24, 28–29, 32, 37, 61, 75, 81, 116, 153, 167, 170, 173; *Toronto Sun* Syndicate: 2–3, 30, 38, 62, 64, 72–73, 93, 95, 98, 105, 120–21, 144, 168, 171, 175–77, 180, 182–83; Boris Spremo private collection: 106; Paul White private collection: 16.